L'AFFAIRE PETRAEUS

The Benghazi Stand-down and the Plot to "Carterize" Obama

Wayne Madsen

Copyright ©2012 by Wayne Madsen

All rights reserved. No part of this publication may be reproduced, stored in a retrieval system, or transmitted in any form or by any means, electronic, mechanical, photocopying, recording, or otherwise, without the prior permission of the author.

WMR is the news and views website WayneMadsenReport.com.

ISBN: 978-1-300-48383-0

Table of Contents

Introduction	4
Chapter 1 – Sex, Lies, and Audiotapes	8
Chapter 2–Paula Broadwell: La Femme Fatale?	26
Chapter 3 – By Dawn's Early Light	37
Chapter 4 – Petraeus's Predecessors and CIA Games	48
Chapter 5 – Karl Rove, again!	58
Chapter 6 – Benghazi: A foreign "false flag" attack?	68
Chapter 7 – Petraeus: A general with little respect from his troops	88
Afterword	98
Appendix	107
Index	120

Introduction

On November 9, 2012, retired General David Howell Petraeus, the 22nd director of the Central Intelligence Agency, stunned Washington's power corridors and the rest of the world by announcing he was resigning over an extramarital affair. The general who was beloved by neo-conservatives like John McCain and neo-liberals like Barack Obama, Jr. left his admirers stunned by the circumstances of his resignation and the sudden fall from grace of such an idolized figure.

However, for those who had covered past scandals in Washington there was an expectation of more shoes to drop and drop they did. The Friday afternoon news of the Petraeus scandal was connected to a wider military and intelligence crisis arising from the presidential election campaign that was concluded two days prior with the re-election of President Obama. Normally, Friday afternoon press releases and spontaneous resignations are timed in the hope the media will ignore them as they wrap things up for the weekend. It was not to be the case with Petraeus's resignation.

Lauded by both the Bush and Obama administrations for his marshaling of troops in contrived military campaigns in Iraq, Afghanistan, and, in support of the "global war on terror," throughout the Arab and Muslim world, Petraeus had served as the commander of the Multi-National Force for Iraq, the chief of U.S. Central Command (CENTCOM), and the chief of the International Security Force for Afghanistan. He was also mentioned as a possible candidate for president or vice president on the Republican Party ticket in 2012.

Petraeus graduated from West Point in 1974 and soon thereafter married Holly Knowlton, the daughter of General William Knowlton, the superintendent of West Point while Petraeus was a cadet. Petraeus's marriage had lasted 37 years before revelations about his affair became public.

The Washington spin machine claimed that President Obama first heard about Petraeus's affair and his intent to resign on the evening of November 8, 2012. However, a few weeks before, Petraeus attended a Canadian embassy screening of the movie "Argo," which depicted the CIA's rescue of Americans in Tehran during the U.S. embassy siege.

Petraeus was said by several other attendees to be preoccupied with other matters and totally disinterested in the film that received kudos from current and former CIA rank-and-file. Ironically, it was the Argo operation that preceded President Jimmy Carter's failed attempt to rescue than negotiate a deal with Iran to have the hostages released. Romney was trying to bring about a "Jimmy Carter" scenario to create a major international crisis for Obama that would serve as his "October Surprise."

There was a belief by many in the intelligence community that Petraeus's affair was already known to the White House weeks before its public revelation but that it was decided that Petraeus would not make his resignation public until after the November 6 election.

The delay would avoid another scandal on top of the still-festering aftermath of the attack by insurgents on a U.S. compound in Benghazi, Libya, likely an intelligence support facility operated by the CIA, on September 11, 2012, a date which has been burned into the memories of every American. Petraeus's resignation also fed the rumor mill that the extramarital affair scandal, resignation, and the siege of the U.S. compound were somehow linked.

Even before the scandal broke, Petraeus's paramour, Paula Broadwell, the co-author along with *The Washington Post's* Vernon Loeb, of Petraeus's biography titled *All In: The Education of General David Petraeus*, had been under investigation by the FBI for trying to access Petraeus's e-mail. The FBI, according to some media reports, has indicated that neither Petraeus nor Broadwell, who also served as an Army Reserve Lieutenant Colonel and is a married West Point graduate with two sons, faced criminal charges. On my website, WayneMadsenReport.com (WMR), I reported in the past that Loeb was a frequent target of National Security Agency (NSA) surveillance as a result of his publication of leaks, authorized or otherwise, from intelligence sources.

After first meeting Petraeus in 2006 at the Kennedy School of Government at Harvard University, Broadwell traveled several times to Afghanistan where she was "embedded" with Petraeus's units. Broadwell also studied Arabic. She taught at West Point, served as a research staffer at Harvard's Center for Public Leadership, and was working on her PhD at King's College in London when the affair with Petraeus went public.

Chief among Petraeus's defenders was the chair of the Senate Intelligence Committee, Senator Dianne Feinstein (D-CA). Arizona Republican Senator John McCain, who had called Petraeus "my dear General Petraeus," also felt Petraeus should have stayed on at the CIA.

However, Petraeus had his enemies, as well, and many were from within his own ranks. Petraeus's first combat command was not until after he was a general at the age of 50 when he was put in command of the 101st Airborne Division in Iraq in 2003. Prior to that time, Petraeus was called a "pencil sharpener" general, having mainly served on staffs and attending Princeton for his PhD and Georgetown University. In 2004, Petraeus became the first commander of the Multi-National Security Transition Command-Iraq (MNSTC-I) and was responsible for training Iraqi police, army, and security service personnel. Under his command, thousands of U.S. weapons were lost and many ended up in the hands of Iraqi insurgents. There were also questionable contracts awarded to U.S. and Iraqi businesses, such as Custer Battles and Blackwater, firms that had close links to top Republicans.

It was also reported that in Iraq, Petraeus was known as "King David," however, the appellation had little to do with his royal persona and more to do with his fealty to the neo-cons and Israel. One of Petraeus's chief backers was the late Democratic Representative Tom Lantos of California, an arch-supporter of Israel.

Petraeus re-wrote Army counter-insurgency doctrine, which became known as the Petraeus Doctrine. Two words sum up the Petraeus Doctrine: surges and drones.

Although it is too early to ascertain why the FBI was investigating Broadwell, there was some informed speculation from intelligence professionals that the Mitt Romney campaign had inside help from the Pentagon and CIA in arranging for a Jimmy Carter-like "October Surprise" to deny Obama a second term. It was the Iran hostage situation in 1980 and a Reagan-Bush mole inside the National Security Council who tipped off the Republicans about last-minute negotiations between Carter's team and Iran to release the U.S. hostages. The failure of the plan to release the hostages prior to the election ultimately cost

Carter re-election. The name of the White House mole was Robert Gates, on loan from the CIA to the White House. Gates was a loyalist of former CIA director George H. W. Bush. At CIA headquarters in Langley, the question was being asked: Was Petraeus another Gates? And if so, what went wrong for Petraeus to be exposed?

Petraeus, with his close connections to the GOP and the neo-cons, may have attracted the wrong type of girlfriend. Broadwell's access to classified CIA information about the CIA's operations in Benghazi before and after the compound siege raised a number of questions, especially with Petraeus's boss, the Director of National Intelligence retired General James Clapper.

When the FBI was ordered to plug leaks about the Benghazi situation, the bureau began discovering some leaks were coming from high-level CIA sources, possibly including Petraeus via Broadwell.

L'Affaire Petraeus is merely the tip of an iceberg. Below the surface of the Petraeus scandal lie a number of other stories: the militarization of the CIA, the over-reliance on Patraeus's favorite drone technology by U.S. intelligence and the defense establishment, the presence of insurgents within the highest echelons of the officers' corps, and out-of-control commands like the U.S. Central and Africa Commands. The following chapters will unpeel the onion layers and the acrid information that comes with every exposure of the layers of secret and hidden government.

Chapter 1 – Sex, Lies, and Audiotapes

The Washington Post and *The New York Times*, America's designated "newspapers of record" -- false record, it should be added -- began working overtime to spin the Petraeus scandal away from the actual story. There are many details that had not yet emerged and some informed speculation remained the order of the day. However, based on what began to become very clear, a perhaps somewhat unwitting Petraeus; several Republicans, including failed GOP presidential nominee Mitt Romney, Republican Party Svengali Karl Rove, Romney adviser Dan Senor; and the Binyamin Netanyahu government in Israel were involved behind the scenes to discredit and ensure the electoral downfall of President Barack Obama by engineering what Romney and his closest advisers reportedly, themselves, described as a "Jimmy Carter Strategy" in an October Surprise.[1]

The strategy was to bring about an incident in the Middle East that would result in a besieged or overrun U.S. embassy, like the U.S. embassy in Tehran in 1979 and 1980, would result in charges that Obama, like Carter, was weak and ineffectual in dealing with a major crisis. Such a scenario would erase the street credentials Obama pocketed in the "raid" on Osama bin Laden. *Raid* is in quotes because the jury remains out on whether the U.S. Navy SEAL attack on the compound in Abbottabad actually resulted in bin Laden's death or was a staged event to boost Obama's national security resumé. But that is another story for the time being.

The author received confirmation from sources close to the White House that President Obama, in the aftermath of the Benghazi U.S. compound attack, was made aware of a *Seven Days in May*-style plot against him by senior generals and admirals in league with officials of the Romney campaign. The sources stated that President Obama's lackluster performance during the first debate in Denver on October 3, 2012 was due to the fact that he had just been briefed on the conspiracy launched against him by senior members of the military and the CIA. The order went out from the White House for Director of National

---

[1] Craig Unger,"GOP's October Surprise?" Source reveals "Jimmy Carter Strategy" to make Obama seem weak on defense in campaign's final month, *Salon*, October1, 2012.

Intelligence James Clapper and Secretary Panetta to purge the ranks of disloyal officials. And purge they did, at a tempo not seen in modern military history.

It is clear that the plot by the neocons, Romney camp, and elements of the CIA and military failed because key players were already informed of the plans and moved to stop them in their tracks.

Obama's deputy national security adviser and go-to person for intelligence advice, John O. Brennan, the retired CIA official who, while at the agency, helped craft the post-p/11 rendition and torture program (of which Muammar Qaddafi's Libyan intelligence service was a partner), would have known, as would have Panetta, who still had sources within Langley from his own time at the CIA, and Clapper, who sat on the Petraeus affair information until after the election. Brennan's nominal boss, Thomas Donilon would have also been aware of the Benghazi set-up and he would have informed his friend and old boss, Vice President Joe Biden.

The question remains what deputy CIA director Michael Morell knew about the Benghazi stand-down and set-up to embarrass Obama. Much of Morell's experience at the CIA was in Latin American and East Asia-Pacific operations, as well as international energy issues. The fact that Morell not only kept his job but was appointed acting director after Petraeus's resignation is an indication that Morell was not involved with the conspiracy and, in fact, may have been feeding information about it to the White House. It is important to note that the two serious names that were floated to be Petraeus's replacement as director were Morell and Brennan. Rather than being rivals, Brennan and Morell are close colleagues. If the plot against Obama was not highly compartmentalized, assuredly either Brennan or Morell or both would have discovered it.

Although the compound hostage scenario failed in Benghazi, perhaps Brennan and Morell decided to allow the plotter's back-up plan to play out in an effort to discover all the players. When it was clear Obama would win re-election, then the heads would roll, and roll they did.

The right-wing, which should be called the "wrong wing" since they rarely get anything "right," maintains that Obama ordered a stand-down in Benghazi that cost four Americans their lives. In fact, the right wing meme is exactly the point the Romney campaign was trying to make in embarrassing Obama less than two months before the election. It was the same type of embassy siege crisis strategy used to embarrass Jimmy Carter in the autumn of 1980. It worked against Carter in 1980, it failed against Obama in 2012.

The plot involving "King David" was uncovered on the shores of Galilee

As Americans are always reminded in times of personal political scandals, it's the sex that sells air time and newspapers and L'Affair Petraeus was no different. While the scandal was termed by most of Washington's "punditocracy" as a personal tragedy that destroyed two families, the intelligence angle was totally ignored. The media worked itself into a frenzy over the soap opera aspects of the Petraeus affair.

Broadwell was identified by the corporate media as Petraeus's "biographer," without much mention that her book on Petraeus was a sycophantic effort to paint the general as some sort of super-human figure. Even more atrocious were some of the laudatory academic reviews of *All In*, including the following review excerpt written by Andrew Marble, the founding editor of the peer-reviewed *Asia Policy*:

"That urge to tug on Superman's cape — our innate curiosity almost demands it. What kind of person does it take to influence the course of history? How mortal are the seeming immortals that walk among us? Gen. David Petraeus, the most lionized American general in the post-9/11 period, is one such larger-than-life figure. He has a reputation as a visionary, as a master strategist, tactician, diplomat, economic-development expert, media handler and even public intellectual . . . Even his body seems unbound by human limitations: Over the course of his 37-year career in the army, Petraeus seemed to have shrugged off a major gunshot wound to the chest, a crash landing while skydiving that fractured his pelvis and a bout with prostate cancer . . .

Broadwell's credentials make the book more than just a run-of-the-mill biography. The book is grounded in her Ph.D. dissertation research, which traces key themes in Petraeus's intellectual development — his education, his experience and the influence of key mentors — and examines how he put these intellectual principles to action during his career. Her research and interviews were supplemented with assistance from Loeb, a reporter and editor who has worked for many major U.S. newspapers.

But what will draw readers deep into this book is Broadwell's unprecedented firsthand access to her subject. Petraeus, who has a penchant for reaching out to intellectuals and the media, unexpectedly offered her a front-row seat at what would become the final act of his military career. Over the course of 15 months, Broadwell embedded with Petraeus' headquarters in Afghanistan as well as with units in the field; conducted a wide range of interviews; was given access to Petraeus' private notes, letters and e-mails; and accompanied the four-star general on trips back to Washington." [2]

---

[2] Andrew Marble, "All In: The Education of David Petraeus: Review," *The Washington Independent Review of Books*, < http://www.washingtonindependentreviewofbooks.com/bookreview/all-in-the-education-of-david-petraeus/>

Whether the reviewer of Broadwell's tome knew it or not at the time, the attractive "biographer" did have "unprecedented firsthand access to her subject." And Broadwell's front-row seat" to Petraeus's "final act" was to be the end of not only the larger-than-life general's military career but any plans he had for a political career.

Of course, powerful men have been known to elevate the credentials of their mistresses. When former Vice President Nelson Rockefeller died of a heart attack suddenly at his Manhattan townhouse on January 26, 1979, at the age of 70, he was said to have been in the company of a young female aide, Megan Marshack. Rockefeller spokespersons described Marshack as Rockefeller's "art adviser." An Art adviser, a biographer, or just a standard mistress, the English language can be a wonderful device for the rich and powerful.

After news broke of Broadwell's identity and revelation of a two-way spat between Broadwell, who referred to Petraeus as "Peaches," and Arabic-speaking Lebanese-American Jill Kelley, a "close" Petraeus friend who worked as an "unpaid liaison" officer between the State Department and the Joint Special Operations Command at MacDill Air Force Base in Tampa, the news cameras were parked outside Broadwell's home in Charlotte, North Carolina and Kelley's home in Tampa. Every television reporter staking out the two homes must've had visions of themselves being plucked from obscurity, as was lawyer-commentator Greta van Susteren from her commentary on the O. J. Simpson case, and obtain a national television show.

And who could have forgotten that what helped to sink Carter in 1980 was the continuation of ABC News's "America Held Hostage: Day [fill in the blank from 1 to 444]." It reminded Americans, particularly President Carter, every night, like Chinese water torture, that American diplomats and military personnel were being held hostage in Tehran. "America Held Hostage" paid off for anchor Ted Koppel. His nightly hostage reminder morphed into the long-running program "Nightline." How many Fox News and CNN reporters were hoping for a similar career bonanza from a Benghazi hostage situation up to Election Day? Judging from the hype on the two networks over "Benghazi" Romney and his aides were not alone in trying to make a mountain out of a molehill.

It is perhaps fitting that the man referred to as "King David" by his detractors would have seen the plot against Obama unravel on the shores of the Sea of Galilee. Petraeus's former spokesman, retired Army Colonel Steve Boylan, hired by Petraeus to deal with the media in the, may have unwittingly let the cat out of the bag by describing the time line of Petraeus's affair with Broadwell. Boylan said Petraeus's affair with Broadwell, with who he appeared to fancy "sex under the desk," according to emails between the two, began nine or ten months before he ended it four months ago. Using Boylan's math, which obviously came from his friend Petraeus, it means the affair ended in July of 2012 but began around October 2011. Petraeus was sworn in as CIA director on September 6, 2011.

We also know that according to Republican Representatives Dave Reichert (R-WA) and House Majority Leader Eric Cantor (R-VA), a preliminarily unidentified FBI agent leaked the Petraeus affair story, first to Reichert. Then Reichert, instead of following up himself with FBI director Robert Mueller or Attorney General Eric Holder, informed Cantor. Cantor's chief of staff, Steven Sombres, it was reported, phoned the FBI on October 31, 2012 to tell them about the conversation that Cantor had with the FBI "leaker."[3]

Sombres and Cantor's deputy chief of staff Doug Heye have been identified as key players in the FBI leak story. However, they were also identified as FBI targets in an event that took place a little less than two months before Petraeus became CIA director. Cantor led an 80-member House congressional delegation (CODEL) to Israel in August 2011. On the evening of August 18, 2011, members of Cantor's staff, and some thirty Republican Representatives were involved in a skinny-dipping incident at the David Citadel Hotel in Tiberias on the Sea of Galilee. The CODEL was funded by the American Israel Educational Foundation, a branch of the American Israel Public Affairs Committee (AIPAC).[4]

Representative Kevin Yoder (R-KS) was identified as one of the skinny dippers. Also participating in the late night bathing were Sombres, Tim Berry, chief of staff for GOP Majority Whip Kevin McCarthy (R-CA); Laena Fallon, Cantor's former press aide; and Emily Murray, a top policy aide to McCarthy. Several congressmen and their aides reportedly got drunk at the hotel before they jumped into the sea. Joining the swim party were Representatives Steve Southerland (R-FL) and his daughter; Tom Reed (R-NY) and his wife; Ben Quayle (R-AZ), Jeff Denham (R-CA), and Michael Grimm (R-NY).

The FBI agent assigned to investigate alleged threatening emails sent by Broadwell to Kelley was reported by *The Wall Street Journal* to have been the same FBI "employee" who leaked details of the Petraeus matter to Reichert and then to Cantor.[5] The story of the agent began to fall apart as the *Journal* later reported that the FBI agent became obsessed with Kelley and sent shirtless

---

[3] Scott Shane and Eric Schmitt,"E-mails from biographer to a Third Party Led to Petraeus," *New York Times*, November 12, 2012.

[4] Jennifer Steinhauer, "Boehner says Cantor Reprimanded Members Over Galilee Swim," *New York Times*, August 20, 2012.

[5] Evan Perez, Siobhan Gorman, and Devlin Barrett, "FBI Scrutinized on Petraeus," *The Wall Street Journal*, November 12, 2012.

photos of himself to her.[6] In the world of intelligence, such extraneous information is termed "clutter" and is designed to blur the actual facts.

The FBI agent friend of Jill Kelley was later identified as Frederick W. Humphries, 47 and married. Assigned to Tampa, he was described as "obsessive" in pursuit of Arab and Muslim terrorist suspects. In other words, he fit the bill of an Islamophobe and blended in nicely with the cabal that was out to set up Obama in an October Surprise.. It was Humphries who sent "shirtless" photos of himself to Kelley, described by Humphries' de facto union general counsel Lawrence Berger, of the Federal Law Enforcement Officers' Association, as a "joke."[7] Kelley was described as a liaison between CENTCOM and the representatives of various Middle East nations. Saudi Arabia, and Qatar, both involved in supporting the Libyan rebels who attacked the U.S. compound in Benghazi, had officers assigned to CENTCOM at MacDill Air Force Base. After the scandal broke, Kelley had her "Friends of MacDill" social pass for the base revoked.

Although Humphries allegedly spoke to Reichert in Washington, it was an FBI colleague of Humphries who, according to some sources, spoke to Eric Cantor. The rabbit hole became deeper.

Humphries was a lead agent in the 1999 investigation of Ahmed Ressam, the Algerian national who was convicted of trying to blow up Los Angeles International Airport on New Year's Eve 1999, the so-called "Millennium Bombing." It was another Berger – former National Security Adviser Sandy Berger, who pleaded guilty to stealing from the National Archives in Washington, DC copies of classified documents on internal Clinton administration assessments of the Millennium plot. It was later revealed by the House Government Reform Committee and the Archives that Berger had access to original documents on the Millennium plot and he could have removed, destroyed, or hidden any number of originals without anyone being the wiser.

In 1999, when Humphries was in Seattle investigating the Ressam plot, Reichert was the sheriff of King's County, the seat of which is Seattle. It is quite clear that Reichert and then-Seattle FBI agent Humphries had a relationship in 1999 that continued until Humphries took it upon himself to relay law enforcement sensitive information on Petraeus and Broadwell directly to Reichert, bypassing well-established FBI and Justice Department protocols for liaison with Congress.

---

[6] "Key FBI Agent Identified as Frederick Humphries," *The Wall Street Journal*, November 15, 2012.
[7] Mike Carter, "Shirtless FBI agent: Photo was joke emailed to friends, reporter," *Seattle Times*, November 14, 2012.

In May 2010, Humphries short and killed a military veteran at the main gate at MacDill. The Justice Department and FBI later ruled that Humphries use of deadly force was justified.[8] However, the man shot by Humphries was 61-year old Army veteran Ronald Bullock, a resident of Hampden, Massachusetts, who was staying at MacDill's Family Campground. Bullock apparently got into an altercation at the campground and was leaving the base through the main Dale Mabry Highway gate when Humphries was trying to "secure" the gate. There was never any explanation why an FBI agent was involved in a military security matter on base property, however, Humphries insisted that Bullock charged at him with a knife and Humphries shot him.[9]

The FBI investigated the Galilee incident for possible Israeli intelligence compromise of the House members and their staff. However, the FBI never revealed the outcome of its investigation. It was Heye who announced that Cantor had satisfied the FBI's concerns. If the FBI's investigation continued, other doors may have opened, doors that led to a planned 2012 "October Surprise" against the President -- doors that led to Cantor's involvement with the Romney campaign in staging the October Surprise. Romney's senior foreign policy aide was Dan Senor, who is close to Netanyahu and Cantor.

Broadwell in Israel

Paula Broadwell is a master's degree graduate of the University of Denver's Josef Korbel School of International Studies, named after the father of former Secretary of State Madeleine Albright and the *alma mater* of former Secretary of State Condoleezza Rice, whose mentor was Professor Korbel. The University of Denver, like the University of Chicago, has become a spawning ground for neocon academics. Broadwell's fellowship at Harvard University reportedly included trips abroad to Syria and Iran.[10] Broadwell is also reportedly fluent in Arabic.

Broadwell, in recent years, had also been a frequent visitor to the Persian Gulf, Jordan, and, more importantly, Israel. But even as a West Point cadet, Broadwell spent time in Israel. She admitted in a July 29, 2012 interview that while at West Point, she "was exposed to the Israeli Defense Forces as well as the Palestinian Liberation Organization. I met high level politicians and officials and gained an understanding of the dynamics of life on a communal kibbutz, in a

---

[8] Michael S. Schmidt, Scott Shane, and Alain Delaquérière, "Veteran FBI Agent Helped Start Petraeus E-Mail Inquiry," *New York Times*, November 14, 2012.
[9] "Man shot and killed trying to leave MacDill AFB," WTSP-TV 10 Tampa, May 20, 2010.
[10] Bismarck, North Dakota Century High School-Academics-Paula Broadwell
<http://www.chs.bismarckschools.org/chs/chshof/2006/academics/>

refugee camp, and in a Bedouin village, having 'embedded' within each community."[11]

Broadwell, in the same interview, stated that she conducted "surveillance on the DMZ in Korea, providing conflict resolution training in Africa . . . [participated in] document exploitation against war criminals in Bosnia, jumping out of airplanes to earn Thai, Indian, and Czech parachute wings, putting together infiltration plans for special forces commandos, serving undercover with the FBI."[12] Broadwell also had close connections with the neo-conservative "think tank" industry in Washington, having served as a deputy director of the pro-Israeli Jebsen Center for Counter-Terrorism at Tufts University, an entity that churns out pro-Israel and other neo-con talking points for America's elected and appointed government leaders.

In other words, if Broadwell can be believed, she had all the street credentials required of an American intelligence agent, an intelligent asset who was tasked to write a self-serving book about Petraeus in cahoots with a *Washington Post* editor. The old ties between Langley and the *Post* continue to flourish.

The catalyst that set the Middle East on fire

The suspicious deaths of two national security agents who may have had knowledge of a threat by Israel and the Romney campaign to discredit Obama add to the plot against the President. On May 10, 2012, Secret Service agent Rafael Prieto, a native of Palmdale, California, accompanied President Obama to Los Angeles where he attended the "Starmageddon" fundraiser at the home of actor George Clooney at 151 El Camino in Beverly Hills. Previously, Prieto was assigned to the security detail of former President Bill Clinton and was based out of the White Plains, New York FBI office. A member of the FBI's national security team in Los Angeles was Stephen Ivens. Ivens's wife Thea said that her husband was unable to sleep over something that was causing him to have anxiety attacks.

On the evening of May 10, Ivens, the father of a two-year old son, grabbed his gun at his home on the 700 block of Scott Road in Burbank and went out on foot into the Burbank foothills. Ivens was reportedly distraught and may have been meeting someone. Prieto happened to be in Los Angeles at the same time. On July 20, after a massive search, Ivens's body was found behind a church near his home on the 2600 block of Scott Road in Burbank after two hikers reported a strange odor.[13] However, on the second day of their search, police and the FBI

---

[11] http://www.claudiachan.com/interviews/paula-broadwell/
[12] Ibid.

used dogs that alerted on Ivens's scent in the foothills but never discovered his body. The Los Angeles medical examiner's office, which, over the decades, has issued findings that defy logic, concluded that Ivens's died of a self-inflicted gunshot wound at the scene where his body was discovered some three months later.

It is unusual for a Secret Service agent to be transferred from a former President's detail to that of a current President. However, in the case of Prieto, he joined Obama's detail from Clinton's. After a period of frostiness, Obama and Clinton patched up past differences and Clinton became one of Obama's chief campaign surrogates. If Obama was made aware of a plot against him by senior military and intelligence officers, he may have confided in Clinton who, after the Monica Lewinsky affair, would have asked Obama how trustworthy his Secret Service detail was. Clinton's experience with FBI White House liaison Gary Aldrich, who, in 1996 wrote *Unlimited Access: An FBI Agent Inside the Clinton White House,* which exposed Clinton to charges of national security lapses, made the ex-President a believer in trust of the security detail. If Obama expressed any reservations about his security, Clinton may have suggested Prieto and a transfer from New York to the White House may have been arranged.

On the evening of October 27, Prieto's body was discovered in his car in the Mount Pleasant neighborhood of northwest Washington, DC. It was reported that Prieto left the engine of his car running in an alley at 19th and Kenyon Streets and that he died from carbon monoxide poisoning. WMR was informed that a DC policewoman was taking photographs of homes across the street from Prieto's residence, which he shared with another Secret Service, on the 1900 block of Kenyon Street. The policewoman was photographing the homes after Prieto's body was discovered. If Prieto died from what was already concluded to be a suicide, why were the DC Metropolitan Police interested in nearby homes. The DC police had also roped off the intersections of 19th and Kenyon Street and Kenyon Street and Adams Mills Road during a suicide investigation that involved a dozen DC police cars and a crime scene mobile unit and unidentified trucks.

Prieto was said to be despondent after he was discovered to have had a six-year affair with a Mexican woman. Prieto was identified by another Secret Service agent who was under investigation for a scandal involving Secret Service agents on Obama's detail in Cartagena, Colombia and prostitutes during the Summit of the Americas last April. WMR reported at the time that the compromising of the Secret Service agents was part of a plot by Netanyahu and

---

[13] Jason Kandel, "Police Recover Body of Missing FBI Agent, NBC News 4 Los Angeles, November 14, 2012.

Mossad operatives, the latter running the prostitution racket in Cartagena, to discredit Obama.

A few weeks after the Cartagena scandal broke, Prieto and Ivens were in Los Angeles during the Obama fundraiser where another plot was being hatched, one that would create a firestorm in the Middle East and lead to the 9/11/12 attack on the U.S. diplomatic compound in Benghazi, Libya by Ansar al-Sharia guerrilla forces. The U.S. compound attackers were associated with Al Qaeda, the always-reliable entity that comes to the propaganda assistance of the neocons every time American national security is placed on the sacrificial altar of the "Temple of Treason."

A 13-minute long trailer for an anti-Islamic film called "The Innocence of Muslims," which depicted the Prophet Mohammed as a sex pervert, was ready to be released on YouTube as the match that would set alight the Middle East. The trailer was filmed the year before as "Desert Warriors" and was the project of an odd consortium of Egyptian Coptic Christians, Hollywood porn movie producers who are largely Jewish. Involved in the production were Robert Brownell, aka Alan Roberts, of Tarzana, California, and a real estate developer named Jimmy Israel.[14] Brownell, who used a number of porn actors in the movie who were told that the main character was "George" and not Mohammed, has produced such "classics" as *The Sexpert* and *The Happy Hooker Goes to Hollywood*.

Both Roberts and Israel were associated with Egyptian-American Copts named Sam Bacile, whose real name is Nakoula Basseley Nakoula (Screen Actors Guild name Abnob Nakoula Basseley), and Joseph Nasralla Abdelmasih, an anti-Muslim who runs Media for Christ and has connections to anti-Muslim Zionist activists Pam Geller, Robert Spencer, and David Horowitz. Other players in the film production were Steven Klein and Gary Cass, both anti-Muslim Christian fundamentalist activists. At about the same time that Cantor was hosting 80 members of the House in Israel, courtesy of AIPAC, and Petraeus and his paramour Broadwell were taking up residence at Langley, production was underway on the anti-Islamic video being filmed in front of as green screen in Duarte and on the set of what is known as "Baghdad Square," a Middle East war setting located at the Blue Cloud Film Ranch in Santa Clarita, California. Paramount's television division built the set. Paramount TV is part of CBS, which is owned by arch-Zionist Sumner Redstone.

Tim Dax, one of the film's actors who past film credits included gay films, was previously told by producers he would be playing Samson, the Jewish hero

---

[14] Rocco Castoro, "Who Is Alan Roberts, The Director of *Innocence of Muslims*? We Think His Real Name is Robert Brownell, *Vice*, <http://www.vice.com/read/who-is-alan-roberts-the-director-of-innocence-of-muslims-we-think-his-name-is-robert-brownell>

from Old Testament folklore. Dax said one of his lines was to call the Prophet "Muhammad the bastard," push him into a tent where he would then put his head between a woman's thighs.[15]

Santa Clarita is up Interstate 5 from Ivens's home in Burbank and due southwest on Highway 14 from Prieto's hometown of Palmdale. After the anti-Muslim video was released it was revealed that the FBI Los Angeles office, where Ivens had worked as a national security and counter-intelligence agent, was investigating the producers of the film. However, the FBI did not indicate when the investigation began and whether Ivens was part of the FBI team looking into the backers of the film.

What could Ivens and Prieto have had in common? Prieto's widow is Hollywood film executive Ruth Pomerance, someone who would have been privy to the type of Hollywood gossip that would not normally make its way to Washington and to the Secret Service and FBI.[16] Pomerance worked with the movers and shakers of Hollywood as the former head of Michael Ovitz's Artists Management Group, Executive Vice President for Production and Development at USA Films, and Vice-President of Lee Rich Company in New York. Could she have discovered something about the plan to create an incident that would destroy Obama's chances for re-election and imparted that information to her husband, who was sworn to take even a bullet for the president? Did Prieto share the information on the incendiary film with Ivens, a criminal conspiracy so wide that it caused the FBI agent to suffer from anxiety attacks?

Bacile, who also used the aliases Nicola Bacily and Erwin Salameh, claimed to be an Israeli-American. Bacile claimed he received funding for the film project from 100 Jewish donors. After Bacile was identified as Egyptian Coptic, AIPAC and the Anti-Defamation League immediately denounced the reports on Bacile's Jewish connections with the hackneyed "anti-Semitic" refrain. However, it cannot be denied that the "Innocence of Muslims" project involved Jews long associated with Hollywood. And there is a possibility that Ivens and Prieto were both aware of the plot to release the anti-Islam trailer by circles that had been associated with the Republican and military officers' plot against Obama.

Benghazi: the aborted attempt to create a Jimmy Carter Strategy hostage situation

The attempt to create what Romney called a "Jimmy Carter Strategy" at the U.S. diplomatic compound in Benghazi was immediately seized upon by Fox News,

---
[15] Jens Erik Gould, "The Making of *Innocence of Muslims*: One Actor's Story," *Time*, September 13,.2012.
[16] Jonathan Allen, "Secret Service agent in affair probe found dead," *Politico*, November 1, 2012.

the Romney campaign, and neocon talking heads as a demonstration of Obama's poor leadership when faced with a crisis. Romney's attempt during the second debate with Obama to claim that the president never used the term terrorism to describe the attack on the consulate that killed Ambassador Christopher Stevens, Foreign Service Information Management officer Sean Smith, and ex-US Navy SEAL team and likely CIA non-official cover security contractor agents Glen Doherty and Tyrone Woods. The two ex-SEALs were said to work for a little-known security firm called the Blue Mountain Group. Why was Stevens being protected by contractors in a dangerous war zone? Was it because certain elements within the CIA who were loyal to Petraeus could not be trusted to ensure Stevens's safety? Was Stevens a sacrificial lamb all along in order to embarrass Obama?

It was reported that three news organizations, the Associated Press, *The New York Times* and *The Washington Post*, were aware that Doherty and Woods were CIA agents but withheld reporting the connection after receiving a request from the government. ABC News did not sit on the information and reported: "Glen Doherty, a 42-year-old former Navy SEAL who worked as a contractor with the State Department, said he personally went into the field to track down so-called MANPADS, shoulder-fired surface-to-air missiles, and destroy them. After the fall of dictator Moammar Gadhafi, the State Department launched a mission to round up thousands of MANPADS that may have been looted from military installations across the country. U.S. officials previously told ABC News they were concerned the MANPADS could fall into the hands of terrorists, creating a threat to commercial airliners."[17]

The Benghazi compound underwent a five-hour siege that began around 9:42 pm, certainly long enough for the U.S. Navy, U.S. Africa Command (AFRICOM), and CIA to react in time to save the staff. The siege was after nightfall and long after normal protesters would have been gathered outside the compound for optimum television coverage. A flash precedence message called a CRITIC was sent from the compound, likely from Sean Smith, the communications specialist, which alerted the chain of command in Washington that what was being experienced was no mere protest engendered by the anti-Muslim video. Benghazi, unlike the scene at the U.S. embassy in Cairo, was a paramilitary operation by seasoned guerrillas. Stevens, before the siege, met with a Turkish envoy, who also served as a liaison to the Salafist-supported Libyan rebels. Stevens reportedly was trying to gather up portable shoulder-held missile launchers given by him and the CIA to Libyan rebels for use against Muammar Qaddafi's government. The Libyans were transferring the missile launchers to

---

[17] Lee Ferran, "American Killed in Libya Was on Intel Mission to Track Weapons," ABC News, November 13, 2012.

allies within the ranks of the Turkish-supported Syrian rebels. The Libyan army brigade guarding the U.S. compound was said to have been totally infiltrated by Ansar al-Sharia and Omar Abdul Rahman Brigades guerrillas allied with Al Qaeda.

Moreover, the Libyan Salafist rebel said to have planned the attack on the compound, Osama bin Laden's one-time driver and business associate in Sudan, Sufyan Ben Qumu, was incarcerated by the United States in Guantanamo but was released and handed over to Qaddafi's government in 2007 with the agreement that he would be kept in prison in Libya. However, he was released by Qaddafi in 2010 as part of a special amnesty. Qumu later appeared as a leader of the anti-Qaddafi rebels who were also being supported by NATO, the United States, Israel, Saudi Arabia, the UAE, Qatar, and Turkey.

It is inconceivable that the CIA would not have known about the plan to attack the compound. A month prior to the election, Representative Darrell Issa (R-CA), the chairman of the House Oversight and Government Reform committee who was hoping to make some political hay from the Benghazi attack for the Republicans and Romney, heard testimony from Eric Nordstrom of the State Department's Diplomatic Security Service. Nordstrom stated, "The ferocity and intensity of the attack was nothing that we had seen in Libya, or that I had seen in my time in the Diplomatic Security Service."[18]

Nordstrom was a 14-year veteran of the DSS, a time period that would have included deadly attacks on U.S. diplomatic facilities in East Africa and Yemen. Nordstrom stated he hadn't seen anything a ferocious as the Benghazi attack in 14 years. Surely, the CIA must have had intelligence that it was about to take place, even if one disregards the incendiary anti-Muslim movie clip that triggered violence throughout the Middle East aimed at U.S. diplomatic targets. Did the CIA know about the extent of the attack and in order to carry out the Jimmy Carter Strategy, let it happen on purpose? It's the old LIHOP question that has dogged 9/11 researchers since 2001. And it would rear its ugly head on 9/11 in 2012.

The CIA claimed it did not reveal much about the siege in Benghazi because it didn't want to reveal the extent of the CIA's presence in the city. Intelligence sources and methods were said to be at risk.

In early September, Petraeus made a secretive trip to Istanbul, Turkey where he met with Turkish Prime Minister Recep Tayyip Erdogan and Turkish MIT intelligence chief Hakan Fidan. Unlike Petraeus's earlier trip to Ankara in March,

---

[18] Ray McGovern,"Why To Say No To Susan Rice," *Consortium News*, December 4, 2012.

the CIA chose to meet Turkish officials in Istanbul, a major CIA station that has, in the past, been infiltrated by Mossad moles in the CIA.

The history of the CIA with "Al Qaeda" in Libya is important to note. WMR reported on this relationship on June 5, 2011 after the author returned from Libya during the rebel and NATO attacks on Muammar Qaddafi's forces:

> "The Obama administration may have officially pronounced the assassination by U.Ss Special Operations forces of reputed "Al Qaeda" leader Osama bin Laden in Pakistan but that has not deterred the U.S. administration from providing over two-thousand "Al Qaeda" irregulars with weapons and other support in rebel-controlled eastern Libya.
>
> The "Al Qaeda" guerrillas, Salafists who practice the extremist Wahhabist sect of Islam promoted by Saudi Arabia, the United Arab Emirates, and Qatar -- all three countries members of the anti-Qaddafi Arab front supporting the NATO attack on Libya -- are drawn from Afghanistan, Yemen, Saudi Arabia, Egypt, Algeria, Morocco, and Tunisia, according to a group of Libyan journalists who recently reported from Benghazi and made it back to Tripoli to report on what they witnessed on the ground in rebel-held territory in eastern Libya.
>
> This reporter was shown raw video footage of the Salafists in Benghazi cutting the throat of a Qaddafi supporter and severing his head. The footage was reminiscent of the 'Al Qaeda' beheading in Pakistan of Wall Street Journal reporter Daniel Pearl and American Nick Berg in Iraq. The Libyan journalists asked me why such footage of rebel atrocities is not being aired by CNN, Al Jazeera, or the BBC. I replied, 'corporate control by the western war industry.'
>
> I also saw another video of the wounds sustained by a Libyan nurse in a Benghazi hospital who was horribly disfigured by Salafist guerrillas. The woman's head was cut in several places, her throat was cut, and she had deep gashes in her arms. The Libyan journalists also witnessed other women in Benghazi whose breasts had been cut off by Libyan rebels.
>
> The Libyan media team was in Benghazi while French philosopher Bernard-Henri Lévy was visiting representatives of the rebel National Transitional Council in Benghazi before traveling to Jerusalem. The Libyan journalists reported that Levy told the rebels that if they wanted to see increased support from NATO, they should establish relations with Israel. After Levy met with the rebel commanders, it was announced that if victorious over Colonel Qaddafi's forces, they would proceed to establish diplomatic relations with Israel. Israeli Prime Minister Binyamin Netanyahu confirmed Levy's meeting with the Libyan rebels and the topic of their recognition of Israel.

> *Levy is also a supporter of former International Monetary Fund (IMF) director Dominique Strauss-Kahn. Levy has attacked the credibility of the Guinean chambermaid who charged that Strauss-Kahn sexually assaulted her in the Sofitel Hotel in Manhattan. Levy's friends in the Libyan rebel movement have been charged with raping and killing a number of workers, including women, from black African nations, including Guinea. The rebel racial-motivated attacks on black workers in Libya have resulted in a massive refugee crisis on Libya's borders with Tunisia and Egypt.*
>
> *It was Levy who convinced French President Nicolas Sarkozy to be the first to recognize the Libyan rebels and commit French military force to their assistance. It is now being reported from Brega, a contested city on the battlefront, that French helicopters have entered the Libyan war on behalf of the rebel forces.*
>
> *Sarkozy is said to have received substantial campaign funds for his run for the presidency of France from Qaddafi financial sources. In addition, the loss in 2008 of $1.3 billion dollars of Libyan sovereign wealth funds because of 'bad investments' by Goldman Sachs reportedly involved top officials of the French government and the financial sector, including those close to Sarkozy and Strauss-Kahn, many of whom are French Jews who ardently support Israel and, now, the Libyan rebels.*
>
> *WMR has also learned by informed sources in Tripoli that the former head of Libyan intelligence under Qaddafi, Musa Kusa, was long believed to have been a double agent for the CIA in Libya. Kusa defected to Britain two weeks after the NATO attacks on Libya commenced.*
>
> *Like former Egyptian intelligence chief and vice president Omar Suleiman, Kusa was a regional point man for the CIA's "extraordinary rendition" and torture program that used Middle Eastern nations like Egypt, Libya, Tunisia, Jordan, and Syria as CIA partners."*

Did the siege of the compound involve the CIA's use of some of Kusa's old interrogation centers for torturing rebels to try to recover arms? Or were the so-called Al Qaeda insurgents being paid by the CIA to arrange for a hostage situation when something went radically wrong and four Americans were killed? These are questions that remain to be answered.

Panetta and Joint Chiefs Chairman Martin Dempsey were not informed of the Benghazi siege and the danger to Stevens for a full hour after the CRITIC message was sent from Stevens to the State Department, White House, Pentagon, NSA, and CIA.

Clapper, the former head of the Defense Intelligence Agency, who had reportedly tangled with Petraeus in the past, was said to have learned of Petraeus's extramarital affair at 5 pm on Election Day. Clapper, who oversees the CIA, demanded Petraeus resign. However, it is more likely that Clapper, who, like Panetta and Dempsey, were considered loyal to Obama, realized the nature and extent of the Jimmy Carter Strategy and decided it was important to clean house. Even Clapper was likely not aware that Obama would be re-elected at 5 pm on Tuesday.

The relevant question is what the Turkish envoy told Stevens at their meeting prior to the attack. Did the pro-Salafist Turks demand that Stevens release the Libyan militants and did Stevens refuse? Were the militants a key to the eventual embassy hostage siege that would be used to destroy Obama's presidency? Did Stevens, like Ivens and Prieto know too much? Has Stevens become a liability that could have exposed part of all of the "Jimmy Carter Strategy" against Obama. These are the questions that congressional investigators should ask witnesses, including Petraeus, Broadwell, and Romney under oath. As for Cantor, the House Ethics Committee should begin an immediate investigation of him and his staff, seizing all emails and files and urging Speaker of the House John Boehner to suspend or fire him as Majority Leader during the ethics investigation. The question is not so much what Cantor knew and when he knew it, but why did he know?

Cantor's staffs' contention that the initial report from an FBI "leaker" went to Reichert is dubious. Reichert, a former King's County detective, was a member of the House Homeland Security Committee, not the House Intelligence Committee, which has overall responsibility for the CIA. Reichert was approached by Rep. Jay Inslee (D-WA), now Washington governor-elect, about his mental health following a subdural hematoma after a tree branch struck him on the head in 2010. There were suggestions by his political opponents that Reichert's memory may have been impaired. Reichert insists he is fine but Cantor and his staff would find using Reichert as an initial source for the FBI leak about Petraeus advantageous if the FBI pursues the veracity of Cantor's and his staffs' story.

House Intelligence Committee Chairman Mike Rogers (R-MI) was briefed on the Petraeus affair by the FBI prior to his Senate counterpart Senator Dianne Feinstein (D-CA) being informed. Feinstein has complained about being left out initially but she, like the individual who, after Petraeus's resignation, was being touted as a potential replacement for Petraeus at the CIA, former Representative Jane Harman (D-CA) -- who was under investigation for her links to Mossad agents at the Israeli embassy in Washington -- are known to be virtual sieves of U.S. intelligence to Israeli intelligence agents and non-cleared individuals heading U.S. Jewish organizations like the American Israel Public Affairs Committee (AIPAC).

General Ham was in a position to order assistance from U.S. naval units off Benghazi's coast but failed to do so from his command post at the Pentagon. British intelligence sources in Benghazi claimed Stevens's compound and the CIA annex were under sustained fire by attackers on two separate occasions, without help arriving from a U.S. Special Forces Commander's In Extremis Force or CIF deployed from Stuttgart, Ham's permanent AFRICOM headquarters, to Croatia for OPERATION JACKAL STONE, a training exercise. Information on the CIF in Croatia was leaked by Broadwell in her Denver speech but it was also suspiciously reported by Fox News around the same time.

Romney's role is also key. He appeared to be at the center of the Jimmy Carter Strategy and it is worth noting the involvement of Petraeus and other flag rank officers, including ousted chief General Carter Ham and Rear Admiral Charles Gaouette, the commander of the Middle East-deployed *USS John Stennis* aircraft carrier strike force, in a potentially wider scandal.

Gaouette was sacked by the Navy for "inappropriate leadership judgment" while his carrier group was in the Pacific en route to the Indian Ocean. Although the *Stennis* group was in the Pacific during the U.S. compound siege in Benghazi on September 11, Gaouette's departure had nothing to do with personal misconduct and was very unusual during a deployment.

It is clear that whatever Stevens was involved in had to do with the arming or disarming of radical Islamist guerrillas who were active in Libya and Syria and supported by Turkey and the Gulf Cooperation Council (GCC) countries of Qatar, Saudi Arabia, and the United Arab Emirates. Concurrent with the Petraeus-Broadwell scandal, Navy civilian Arabic linguist James Hitselberger, assigned to an unconventional warfare element that is part of the Joint Special Operations Task Force-Gulf Cooperation Council in Bahrain, was charged with violating the Espionage Act for placing classified documents in a publicly-accessible archive called the "James F. Hitselberger Collection" at the Hoover Institution at Stanford University.

The collection, according to Stanford University, consisted of:

"Broadsides, flyers, leaflets, serial issues, and sound recordings, relating to political conditions in Iran under the reign of the Shah, the Iranian political opposition, the revolution of 1979, post-revolutionary conditions in Iran, and political opposition to the new Iranian regime. Includes many issuances of the People's Mojahedin Organization of Iran and of various

Iranian émigré student groups in the United States and elsewhere, and sound recordings of political demonstrations. Also includes flyers, leaflets, serial issues and photographs relating to the post-2003 insurgency and American military occupation in Iraq, to American military presence in Bahrain, and to Islam."

Like the University of Denver's Korbel School, the Hoover Institution is a nesting- ground for neocons. The timing of the October 26 arrest and indictment of Hitselberger, just as the information about Petraeus and Broadwell began to spread among certain circles in Washington, was suspicious. Hitselberger was described as someone who could, with no money or assets, successfully blend into any environment in any country, especially Arab countries like Libya and Syria. Was Hitselberger trafficking in classified documents to aid and abet the conspirators against Obama? Was he privy to Benghazi cables sent to the U.S. embassies in the Salafist-supporting GCC countries? Or was he aware of the wider conspiracy against Obama and incarcerated to ensure his silence?

One noteworthy postscript to the Hitselberger episode was that he worked from 2004 to 2007 for the Titan Corporation, a subsidiary of intelligence giant L3 Communications, as an Arabic translator in Iraq. Titan was a major player in the detainee torture scandal in Iraq. At the time of his arrest in Kuwait, Hitselberger was working for Global Linguist Solutions LLC, which has not been very open about his mission in traveling from Arab country to Arab country without any visible means of support.[19]

---

[19] John Diedrich, "Ex-Navy Translator Charged With Espionage," *Military.com News*, November 13, 2012.

Chapter 2–Paula Broadwell: La Femme Fatale?

It is clear why Romney hardly ever lauded the military or veterans during the campaign. Romney's Mormon religion was founded upon treason and insurrection against the U.S. government. The day after the deadly attack on the Benghazi compound, Romney condemned Obama's lack of an immediate response to the attack, even though the lack of a response can now be placed at the doorstep of Petraeus, AFRICOM chief General Ham, and the CIA assets in Benghazi. There were reports out of Libya that U.S. assets were airborne near the compound to repel the insurgents' attack in what was called "Feet Dry Over Libya," but that there was a standing order for the forces not to land. Who gave that order? Was it Ham in Washington? Was it Petraeus? Or was it another conspirator in the military or CIA chain-of-command?

It is also suspected that Stevens and his own background may have involved him in covert side assignments for the CIA. Stevens may have been made aware of the use of some CIA and Pentagon assets to plot with Romney against Obama. Stevens, who was said by State Department insiders to have been gay, would have naturally wanted the gay rights-supportive Obama administration to triumph over the retrogressive Republicans and Romney. The killing of Stevens would have eliminated a potential source of information that could have hanged the conspirators and an impediment to proving advanced arms to Syrian rebels from Libyan caches pursuant to the wishes of Ankara, Riyadh, and Doha.

Washington Post fixture Bob Woodward reported that the Romney campaign offered him a "source" with detailed knowledge of the Benghazi attacks during the last week of October. Who may that source have been? A photograph has emerged of Broadwell with Romney campaign strategist Karl Rove on June 11, 2012. They were attending a meeting in Washington, DC of the

National Conference of State Legislatures (NCSL). The NCSL Legislative Leadership Meeting featured as speakers, political pollster Charlie Cook and Education Secretary Arne Duncan, and Rove. Two things were odd about Broadwell attending the meeting. She was in her Army uniform at what was, ostensibly, a civilian gathering. And NCSL has been at the forefront of drafting legislation on enacting laws that govern the technology used for elections and the maintenance of voter rolls. Karl Rove attending such a gathering is like putting a fox in a henhouse. And what drew Broadwell to a conference partly focused on election integrity? Her background is in counter-terrorism and national security.

Woodward's not quite "scoop"

Woodward would surface again in L'Affaire Petraeus. Woodward had a story in the December 3, 2012 *Washington Post* that said Petraus was urged to run for President while he was commander of U.S. forces in Afghanistan by Fox News chief Roger Ailes. The offer was for Petraues to step down and that Ailes would quit his job as President of Fox News to become Petraeus's campaign chief. The offer was personally conveyed to Petraeus in Afghanistan on April 16, 2011 by Kathleen T. McFarland, a national security expert who often appeared on Fox. The offer, which Petraeus rejected at the time, was said to have the backing of Fox chairman Rupert Murdoch.[20]

On December 14, 2011, WMR reported on Petraeus possibly setting up Obama for a "Jimmy Carter-like fall":

> *"Recent major failures of the CIA in its drone operations in the Middle East and Africa have some congressional sources wondering what is afoot with the CIA. Those in Washington with long memories recall how one of President Jimmy Carter's National Security Council staffers, on loan from the CIA, was feeding classified information on the Iran hostage situation, on sensitive negotiations with Tehran that sought a possible 'October Surprise' by Carter to get the U.S. embassy hostages released by the Iranian government prior to the November election. The information was funneled by the staffer to Ronald Reagan's campaign director William Casey and the vice presidential nominee George H. W. Bush. The NSC staffer feeding the information to Casey and Bush was one Robert Gates. Gates would go on to become CIA director under President Bush 41 and Defense Secretary under Bush 43 and Obama.*

---

[20] Bob Woodward, "Fox News chief's failed attempt to enlist Petraeus as presidential candidate, *The Washington Post*, December 3, 2012.

Petraeus's first major failure, Lebanon, involved Hezbollah's exposure of the CIA's agent network in the country. The CIA station chief, Daniel Patrick McFeely, has been outed as the CIA station chief at the U.S. embassy in the Awkar neighborhood of Beirut. Not only was Hezbollah able to out McFeely, who operates as 'official cover' as part of the embassy staff, but they identified his predecessor, Louis Kahi.

By conducting surveillance of meetings at Pizza Huts and Starbucks in Lebanon between CIA case officers and agents, Hezbollah – and their Iranian allies – were able to construct the CIA's network that included over 1000 top Lebanese politicians, academics, medical doctors, journalists, military personnel, and celebrities. Essentially, the CIA's network in Lebanon has been largely rolled up. According to Al Manar television, the code names of the agents, names like Nick, Jim, Youssef, Liza and Jonah, were also exposed.

The U.S. corporate media has refrained from publishing the names of the CIA station chiefs or the cover names of their Lebanese agents.

Almost simultaneous to the Lebanon roll up, Iran announced it discovered a network composed of at least 42 CIA agents in Iran, operatives that worked in nuclear and other scientific centers, the military, biotechnology, and various universities. Iran's chief prosecutor has indicted fifteen of the 42 for espionage on behalf of the CIA. {At this point, it should be noted that Jill Kelley and her sister enjoyed high-level access to CENTCOM and Petraeus, as well as later to the Obama White House. Their connections to Lebanon are noteworthy. After Petraeus's resignation, it was announced by the Pentagon that the Defense Intelligence Agency would institute the Defense Clandestine Service, which would compete with the CIA's own National Clandestine Service in trouble spots like the Middle East].

On November 26, a U.S. air strike killed 24 Pakistani military personnel on the Pakistani border with Afghanistan. The incident, which frayed already poor relations between the United States Pakistan, resulted in the U.S. being expelled from the CIA's Shamsi airbase in Pakistan, one from which drones were launched, with few successes and many failures, against "terror" targets in Pakistan's volatile mountainous frontier region bordering Afghanistan.

The debacle that resulted in the loss of the Shamsi drone base was followed by the biggest intelligence failure to date, the downing by accident or hostile action, of an

> RQ-170 Sentinel 'stealth'-enabled drone over Iran. President Obama was under pressure to launch a commando raid on Iran to retrieve the state-of-the art technology drone or bomb it and its security detail once it was discovered to be in Iranian hands. Obama chose to ask the Iranian to return the drone to the United States, something Tehran has refused to do, without, at the very least, an official apology.
>
> Obama now has on his hands his Jimmy Carter moment and Petraeus has been manipulating all the 'joy sticks' from his perch at Langley. Obama's potential opponents, including arch-neocon and uber-war hawk Newt Gingrich, are now pouncing on Obama as a weak and ineffectual president because he allowed the RQ-170 to fall into the hands of not only the Iranians, but possibly the Russians and Chinese who will attempt to re-engineer what is known as the mysterious "Beast of Kandahar" to leap frog and at least match the United States in stealth drone technology by years.
>
> And just when Obama did not need any more bad news from his problematic CIA director, news came that an Air Force-operated MQ-9 Reaper drone on counter-terrorist and counter-piracy duty in the Indian Ocean crashed and burst into flames on landing at the international airport on Mahe island in the Seychelles. Most Air Force Reapers are remotely-piloted from Nellis Air Force Base in Las Vegas, Nevada.
>
> Why would Petraeus risk his job as CIA director by embarrassing his commander-in-chief? For starters, being Vice President under President Gingrich or President Romney would be a much better job."

It is now clear that Gingrich was trying to embarrass Obama with the loss of the drone in the same manner that Romney would quickly attack Obama over the Benghazi compound siege and four murders of U.S. personnel. What did the two CIA SNAFUs have in common? David Petraeus.

On November 4, 2011, WMR reported Petraeus's meetings with top Republicans in Washington, while he was still serving as Afghanistan commander, about a potential run for the White House against Obama. The tip to the Pentagon on Petraeus's activities came from New York Democratic Congressman Eric Massa, later run out of town amid a contrived office sex scandal.

Woodward of the *Post* is a day late and a dollar short with his Petraeus story. Here's what WMR reported on November 14, 2011:

"[Massa] raised the red flags of treasonous behavior with top Pentagon brass as it became known that General David Petraeus, the commander of CENTCOM and NATO forces in Afghanistan, was meeting with top GOP officials, including former Vice President Dick Cheney, to plot out a run for the White House in 2012 against Petraeus's own Commander-in-Chief."

Massa first told his story about the Petraeus meetings with Cheney and top Republicans to *Esquire* magazine's Ryan D'Agostino, who later wrote:

"On Friday, March 5, 2010, Congressman Eric Massa, whom I had known professionally for a few years, called me and said that he was preparing to announce his resignation from the U.S. House of Representatives . . . Earlier in the year, long before the allegations had been made public, Massa had called me with a potentially huge story: Four retired generals — three four-stars and one three-star — had informed him, he said, that General David Petraeus, the head of U.S. Central Command, had met twice in secret with former vice president Dick Cheney. In those meetings, the generals said, Cheney had attempted to recruit Petraeus to run for president as a Republican in 2012.

The generals had told him, and Massa had agreed, that if someone didn't act immediately to reveal this plot, American constitutional democracy itself was at risk. Massa and I had had several conversation on the topic, each more urgent than the last. He had gone to the Pentagon, he told me, demanding answers. He knew the powerful forces that he was dealing with, he told me. They'd stop at nothing to prevent the truth from coming out, he said, including destroying him. 'I told the official, 'If I have to get up at a committee hearing and go public with this, it will cause the mother of all shitstorms and your life will be hell. So I need a meeting. Now.'" Massa eventually came to the Esquire offices in New York to tell us the Petraeus story. He spoke with the bluster and hyperbole I had seen in him at stump speeches, but he had credibility on this matter — twenty-four years of active service in the Navy, a seat on the House Armed Services Committee, and an increasing voice in the media as a Democrat who would speak with authority about military issues. Still, when he called the possibility that Petraeus could beat Obama in an election a 'coup' and 'treason,' the characterization seemed odd. 'If what I've been told is true — and I believe it is,' he told myself and two colleagues, 'General David Petraeus, a commander with soldiers deployed in two theaters of war, has had multiple meetings with Dick Cheney, the former vice-president of the United States, to discuss Petraeus's candidacy for the Republican nomination for the presidency. And in fact, that's more than a constitutional crisis. That's treason.'"[21]

In retrospect, Bob Woodard, the *Washington Post* editors, K. T. McFarland, and the television news producers who ran the Petraeus presidential ambitions stories on December 3 and 4, two years after Massa's disclosures to *Esquire*, were all as "insane" as Massa. Or maybe, *Esquire* is just a terrible magazine that doesn't do its homework. The latter seems more likely.

According to Massa, when he was the military assistant to the NATO commander, General Wesley Clark, there were standing orders, strictly enforced by Clark and his staff, that anytime members of the media asked about Clark's political plans, there was one standard response: "We cannot discuss that issue." Apparently, Petraeus followed and entirely different playbook when it came to political discussions.

The *Post* published a transcript of the meeting between McFarland and Petraeus and parts of their conversation indicated that Petraeus was not happy that when Fox "went after" Obama, it decided to go after his war, as well, and Petraeus felt that hurt him:

McFarland: I've got something to say to you, by the way, directly from Roger Ailes.

Petraeus: Oh, at . . . with no one else in the room? I hope?

Q: Well, you know. . . . You guys have ears? Or your ears are dead? No. Okay. Here's the . . . what I told Roger . . .

Petraeus: I'm not running. *[Laughs]*

Q: Okay. But I'm going to tell you that Roger Ailes — and I told him I was coming . . .

Petraeus: I love Roger.

Q: I know. And he loves you, and everybody at Fox loves you. So what I'm supposed to say directly from him to you, through me, is first of all, is there anything Fox is doing, right or wrong, that you want to tell us to do differently?

---

[21] Ryan D'Agostino, "Inside the Insane Saga of Congressman Eric Massa," *Esquire*, May 24, 2010.

Petraeus: You know, actually, ask Bret Baier about this, because I actually did say that I thought that. . . . I actually thought, in a sense, sort of the editorial policy of Fox had shifted. Now, that . . .

Q: On the online, or on the news channel?

Petraeus: Well, I only watch the — you know, the. . . . But I mean, it's your stories that are online here. But it just struck me that it was almost as if, because they're going after Obama, they had to go after Obama's war as well, actually. And I told that to Bret when he was out here. That — again, some of it was headlines, but they . . ."[22]

Petraeus and McFarland then spoke about how loyal three senators, called "The Three Amigos," have been to Petraeus. The Three Amigos are Senators McCain. Lindsey Graham (R-SC), and Joe Lieberman (Ind.-CT).

McFarland then broached to offer from Ailes:

"**Q:** Now, the other thing — I know you've only got a minute left — the other thing, which is directly advice to you from Roger Ailes is . . .

Man: You want us to leave, sir? *[Laughter]*

Petraeus: *[Laughs]* I'm not runnin'.

Q: That's not the question at this point. He says that if you're offered chairman, take it. If you're offered anything else, don't take it, resign in six months and run for president. Okay? And I know you're not running for president. But at some point when you go to New York next, you may want to just chat with Roger. And Rupert Murdoch, for that matter.

Petraeus: Well . . . Well, Rupert's after me, as well. Look, I . . . what I have told people is, I truly want to continue to serve my country if it is in a — you know, a quite significantly meaningful position. And there's all of about two of those in the world. You all have really got to shut your mouths — or shut your . . . Yeah, shut your mouths, too.

Q: I'm only reporting this back to Roger. And that's our deal.

Petraeus: And obviously the chairman would be one of them, and there might be one other. But that's about it. And I'm not going to — you know,

---

[22] "Transcript: Kathleen T. McFarland talks with Gen. David H. Petraeus,"*The Washington Post*, December 3, 2012.

don't want to go to NATO meetings for the rest of my life, or fight service budget battles or anything like that.

Q: Can I give you the gossip that I've picked up about all that?

Petraeus: What's that?

Q: I mean, I'm sure you hear better gossip, but I talked to some former chiefs about this very topic. And they said, well, you know, the White House is particularly nervous . . .

Petraeus: Of course they are.

Q: Well, but . . . and here's the thinking: that they're nervous about. . . . They feel that Obama had this mandate. And the mandate — in his own mind. Obama wanted to do Obamacare . . . He wanted to do environment, which is basically controlling all aspects of the economy. And education, which is the future. So he pushed for Obamacare. He got that done. They didn't anticipate 2010 results. But he now is going to lie low and be very centrist so that they win in '12 and they get the other two. Now, what they need — and this is not from the chiefs, this is from political people — and what they need to cement it so that it doesn't get reversed is a third term. And that means 2016, they need to win, the Democrats need to win, and they need to win with their guy. Their kind of guy. So that then you'd have the stuff as locked in place for a generation. Nobody can come in like Reagan came in and reverse."[23]

The transcript represents a conspiracy of sorts. One of President Obama's top generals, referring to his commander-in-chief merely as "Obama," was in a discussion with the Republican Fox News about an offer to back him for a run against Obama in 2012.

Broadwell, who was attaining the kind of female national security television expert status as McFarland, had every reason to hope that her boyfriend would make a run for the White House. Career-wise, all sorts of opportunities would open up for Broadwell.

After the siege of the compound in Benghazi and the killing of the four Americans, Fox News was the first to conclude that the Americans died because of Obama's negligence as commander-in-chief. However, Fox's friend Petraeus was in charge at the CIA and in charge of a sizable number of CIA assets in

---

[23] Ibid.

Benghazi. So, the more reasonable statement would have been that Petraeus's negligence cost the Americans their lives. Petraesus's negligence would definitely not be an issue for Fox if they were working together to tarnish Obama before the election.

Fox also reported after the siege that CIA officials had refused "desperate requests" for help from U.S. personnel under fire in Benghazi. William Kristol, the editor of *The Weekly Standard*, formerly owned by Murdoch's News Corporation, believed the CIA was blaming the White House for not intervening in the Benghazi situation. In a very telling piece, the *Weekly Standard's* blog headline was, "Petraeus Throws Obama Under the Bus."[24] This represents additional proof that a stand-down in Benghazji was ordered but not by the White House but by the CIA and its allies in the military.

Broadwell's loose tongue

Broadwell, in an October 26, 2012, speech at her University of Denver *alma mater* revealed that the CIA was using the Benghazi annex to hold Libyan militants prisoner. It was from this same annex that the CIA dispatched a rescue team to assist Stevens but only 28 minutes before Panetta, Dempsey, Director of National Intelligence James Clapper, and, assuredly, the White House, had been informed of the attack. The CIA vehemently denied that its annex was being used as a black site. However, the CIA has never admitted to any of its black sites around the world. Broadwell's speech came a day before Cantor said he was first tipped off about the FBI investigation of Broadwell's affair with Petraeus.

Broadwell told the gathering in Denver:

"Now, I don't know if a lot of you heard this, but the CIA annex had actually, um, had taken a couple of Libyan militia members prisoner and they think that the attack on the consulate was an effort to try to get these prisoners back. So that's still being vetted.

The challenging thing for General Petraeus is that in his new position, he's not allowed to communicate with the press. So he's known all of this — they had correspondence with the CIA station chief in, in Libya. Within 24 hours they kind of knew what was happening."[25]

---

[24] Scott Shane, "Petraeus's Quieter Style at CIA Leaves Void on Libya Furor, " *The New York Times*, November 2, 2012.

[25] Max Fisher, "Why did Paula Broadwell think the CIA had taken prisoners in Benghazi?" Quoting from Broadwell's remarks transcribed by Blake Hounshell of *Foreign Policy*, *Washington Post*, November 12, 2012.

Broadwell's knowledge of a classified black site in Benghazi raised suspicions about what in the way of classified information was later discovered by the FBI on her home computer after it was seized by bureau agents with Broadwell's permission.

Petraeus was probably faced with two choices: resigning in disgrace over his "affair" or being prosecuted for treason. He and, presumably others, like Ham and Gaouette, took the easy way out and resigned. Their oath upon being commissioned is succinct:

> *I do solemnly swear (or affirm) that I will support and defend the Constitution of the United States against all enemies, foreign and domestic; that I will bear true faith and allegiance to the same; and that* **I will obey the orders of the President of the United States** *and the orders of the officers appointed over me, according to regulations and the Uniform Code of Military Justice.*

Under Article 90 of the Uniform Code of Military Justice, during times of war – and we are always told we are in a permanent war on terrorism – a military member who willfully disobeys a superior can be sentenced to death. Petraeus is hoping to be named President of Princeton University rather than face a firing squad.

Petraeus has a chance to clear his name to a degree. Just as Marine Corps General Smedley Butler was approached by treasonous Republicans who wanted to oust President Franklin Roosevelt in a coup in 1934, playing along with the plotters until he could amass enough evidence to rat them out to the Congress, Petraeus is in a position to identify the treasonous plotters of 2012. They obviously include Cantor, Rove, Romney, Ham, and others who are, as yet, unidentified. If Petraeus remains silent, he will forever be known by his other handle given to him by his military subordinates: "General Betray Us."

But Petraeus would be no Butler but would tread on the same perilous path already walked upon by General Douglas MacArthur in challenging his own Commander-in-Chief, President Harry S Truman, in 1948.

In 1948, MacArthur, still on active duty and in charge of the American military occupation of Japan, allowed his name to be placed on the Republican Party primary ballots in Wisconsin and Nebraska, in effect, challenging his own commander-in-chief for the presidency. The drafters of the Uniform Code of Military Justice (UCMJ), who were completing work on what would become the criminal code for members of the military in 1948, had MacArthur's political challenge to Truman in mind when they stipulated that such activity by a uniformed military subordinate of the commander-in-chief violated military regulations. When Petraeus sat down with senior Republicans and Fox News employees to discuss a presidential run against President Obama, he was in violation of the UCMJ. However, unlike MacArhur, Petraeus did not simply "fade away," but went on to head the CIA where more plotting against Obama could take place.

Chapter 3 – By Dawn's Early Light

By Dawn's Early Light was the last Cold War movie about renegade Pentagon generals acting without the authorization of the President of the United States. Although the Cold War is long since over, the concept of renegade Pentagon flag rank officers defying the president appears to have become a reality. And every dawn's early light now brings forth new revelations of what can only be described as a major conspiracy to create a foreign conflagration that would see President Obama defeated for re-election amid an engineered crisis in Libya.

As the David Petraeus scandal and the plot against Obama by neocon flag rank officers working with the Mitt Romney campaign continues to unfold, President Dwight Eisenhower's warning about the inherent dangers of the "military-industrial complex" to our democratic form of government becomes as clear as ever:

> "In the councils of government, we must guard against the acquisition of unwarranted influence, whether sought or unsought, by the military-industrial complex. The potential for the disastrous rise of misplaced power exists and will persist.
>
> We must never let the weight of this combination endanger our liberties or democratic processes. We should take nothing for granted. Only an alert and knowledgeable citizenry can compel the proper meshing of the huge industrial and military machinery of defense with our peaceful methods and goals, so that security and liberty may prosper together."

The attempt by senior military members working with the Romney campaign to implement what Romney called a "Jimmy Carter Strategy" to present Obama with a full-scale U.S. embassy hostage situation in Benghazi was not limited to senior military officers and Romney operatives like Dan Senor and Karl Rove but also included the "industrial" portion of Eisenhower's dreaded military-industrial complex.

And down they go, all in a row

Shortly after Petraeus announced that he was resigning over an extra-marital affair, Christopher Kubasik, the incoming chief executive officer of Lockheed-Martin, America's largest defense contractor and which is based not far from the Pentagon in Bethesda, Maryland, was fired by the corporation's board for having a "lengthy, close, personal relationship" with a subordinate employee. With much of the military's functions being contracted out to companies like Lockheed-Martin, a global plot against the President by senior military commanders would have required contractor support. And Lockheed-Martin (or "Lock-Mart") is the biggest and most powerful of them all, with its hooks inside the FBI surveillance and counter-surveillance technology through its ownership of Sandia National Laboratories in New Mexico and contracts for cyber-security at the National Security Agency (NSA) at Fort Meade, Maryland and the FBI at Quantico, Virginia.

Following the Petraeus resignation and Kubasik's firing for the exact same official reason – extramarital affairs – Microsoft's media shy executive for Windows development, Steven Sinofsky, resigned (or as some suggest, was fired by CEO Steve Ballmer). No official reason was given. However, as the Petraeus scandal unfolded and began to involve other senior generals, it also became clear that e-mails between Petraeus and his girlfriend Army Reserve Lieutenant Colonel Paula Broadwell, between Broadwell and a MacDill Air Force Base, Tampa socialite named Jill Kelley, and between Kelley and commander of U.S. and NATO forces in Afghanistan Marine Corps General John Allen were being leaked. It was also reported that the FBI was searching Broadwell's home in Charlotte, North Carolina after reports surfaced that her reported access to classified information did not come from CIA director Petraeus but from another source, or, perhaps, through a backdoor in software provided by Microsoft to the military and intelligence community – a backdoor that now ex-Windows guru Mr. Sinofsky might have known about.

Former NSA and CIA director Michael Hayden, who arranged for Microsoft back doors to be installed in government and commercial software, publicly called for Petraeus to answer questions about the siege of the U.S. embassy and the killing of Ambassador Stevens and three other State Department personnel. However, Hayden, an adviser to Romney, hoped to use the Benghazi attack as a way of diminishing Obama's crisis reaction skills. And, hypocritically, Hayden's backyard was not entirely clean in the extramarital affairs department. Hayden, as NSA director, would have worked closely with Sinofsky and his staff to place back doors into Microsoft Windows e-mail and other communications systems. In fact, Microsoft maintains a full-time office at NSA headquarters to deal with surveillance issues that arise with Microsoft systems.

FBI agents searching Broadwell's home in Charlotte were seen carrying out a Dell PC in addition to an iMac and a printer. It was also emerged that Broadwell appeared in a commercial for a Swiss automatic weapons manufacturer, KRISS Arms, which has its U.S. headquarters in Virginia Beach, Virginia, a city that has close connections to the former Blackwater USA and which is a major base for the Navy SEALS.

Earlier reports that Broadwell sent Kelley threatening e-mails over what Broadwell believed were Kelley's amorous intentions toward Petraeus, now appear to have been false. In fact, a mysterious FBI agent who was in contact with Representatives Reichert and Cantor, appears to have interjected himself into the Petraeus matter but also began sending shirtless photographs of himself to Kelley, a Lebanese-American from Philadelphia who is married to a Tampa surgeon who worked at the Moffitt Cancer Center.

It was leaked from government sources – obviously by the U.S. Attorney's Office in Tampa – that some 30,000 pages of e-mail correspondence between Kelley and General Allen, who succeeded Petraeus as commander in Afghanistan – were obtained by FBI investigators. Allen, who commanded the International security Force in Afghanistan, was slated to become the Supreme Allied Commander of NATO but that nomination was put on hold and investigators were determining the nature of the relationship between Allen and Kelley and whether Kelley obtained classified information from Allen. In January 2013, the Pentagon cleared Allen of any wrongdoing but refused to make public the 20,000 to 30,000 emails. Kelley supposedly worked as an unpaid liaison between the U.S. Central and Special Operations Commands in Tampa and the U.S. State Department and the local community. Kelley reportedly also worked with Vice Admiral Robert Harward, a Navy SEAL and the deputy commander of CENTCOM in Tampa. It should be noted that Petraeus served as chief of CENTCOM before being assigned to Afghanistan to command U.S. and NATO forces.

Allen's deputy commander for logistics in Afghanistan, Brigadier General Jeffrey A. Sinclair, was relieved of his duties in May 2012, just before the FBI found out about Petraeus's affair and around the time that the anti-Islam video began making its rounds.. Sinclair faced charges at Fort Bragg, North Carolina that he engaged in sex crimes against five women: four subordinates and a civilian. The fact that such a case involving a flag rank officer went to a full court-martial is considered highly unusual. In many cases, such cases involving senior officers result in an early retirement and letters of reprimand. However, in a period of disloyal flag ranks officers being discovered throughout commands around the world, what was unusual soon appeared to be standard operating procedure.

About the same time that Petraeus's affair was being circulated to a few individuals in Washington, the Navy relieved Rear Admiral Gaouette of his duties as commander of the *USS Stennis* Strike Group while it was in transit in the Pacific en route to Indian Ocean waters.

And it was not merely Gaouette who was the only high-ranking naval officer canned in a short period of time. Just weeks before they were to receive new commands, the commanding officers of the *USS Mount Whitney*, Captain Ted Williams, and *the USS Fort McHenry*, Commander Ray Hartman, were relieved due to what the Navy reported was "misconduct" for personal reasons.[26] Both ships, the amphibious command ship *Mount Whitney* and the amphibious dock-landing ship *Fort McHenry* were assigned to the Mediterranean Sixth Fleet headquartered in Naples, Italy and both ships were in zone to assist the besieged Benghazi compound on September 11.

It was unusual for the Navy to announce the firing of two Sixth Fleet ship commanders the very same day, November 19, 2012. The investigation of Captain Williams began on October 26, the day before Cantor was told about the Petraeus affair by FBI agent Humphries and the same day the Navy made an arrest in a leak of classified classified documents from its base in Bahrain.

At the time of the Petraeus revelations, it was announced that four-star General William E. "Kip" Ward, the former African-American head of AFRICOM, has been stripped of a star and forced to retire as a three-star general for lavish spending, including an expensive layover in Bermuda, and accepting gratuities, including free Broadway show tickets for him and his wife, from a

---

[26] Cristina Silva, "Navy fires two more commanders," *Stars and Stripes*, November 20, 2012.

defense contractor. General Martin Dempsey, the Chairman of the Joint Chiefs, urged Defense Secretary Panetta to allow Ward to retire as a four-star general, but Panetta ordered the reduction in rank that will cost Ward an estimated $30,000 a year in retirement pay. Ward's scheduled retirement in April 2011 was delayed until a full investigation was conducted on his spending habits during his assignment as the first chief of AFRICOM.

There was an unusual foreign connection to Jill Kelley. The Lebanese-American MacDill Air Force base "socialite" was also the honorary counsel for the Republic of Korea in Tampa. Kelley represented South Korea until the government in Seoul found that the unwanted media attention was too much. South Korea terminated Kelley's honorary consul status after New York businessman Adam Victor accused Kelley of incompetence in brokering business deals with South Korean companies.

On November 27, Kelley and her attorney, Abbe Lowell, a high-powered Washington DC attorney who represented President Bill Clinton in the Monica Lewinsky scandal, Condit in the Chandra Levy matter, and former Senator and Vice Presidential candidate John Edwards in his federal prosecution in matters related to his affair with Rielle Hunter, fought back against certain parties.

Lowell sent a letter to Victor, who claimed Kelley attempted to broker a $3 billion oil and natural gas deal between Victor and four South Korea firms, Samsung, Hyundai, GS and GK, in return for an $80 million commission, 2 percent of the deal, for Kelley. The letter was a cease and desist warning that stated, "If you want to continue seeking publicity for yourself, that is one thing . . . However, if you do that by maligning a person, that is something else." In a letter to the assistant U.S. Attorney for the Middle District of Florida in Tampa, W. Stephen Muldrow, Lowell warned him about leaks that violated privacy laws. Lowell wrote, "You no doubt have seen the tremendous attention that the Kelleys have received in the media . . . All they did to receive this attention was to let law enforcement know that they had been the subjects of inappropriate and potentially threatening behavior by someone else." [See page 118] Lowell was pointing the finger at Muldrow for leaking the information to the media. In a third letter to the Florida Bar, Lowell complained about Kelley's former attorney, Tampa attorney Barry Cohen, for violating attorney-client privilege for talking to the media during the height of the scandal about a conversation Cohen had with Kelley about her relationships with various top military officers.[27]

In addition to Vice Admiral Harward, Kelley was on good terms with General James Mattis, the CENTCOM commander who replaced Petraeus. Kelley attended at least one reception at Mattis's home in Tampa. [see page 117] It was later announced that Mattis was being replaced as CENTCOM chief by General Lloyd Austin.

Kelley also attempted to claim diplomatic immunity by trying to convince Tampa police to move inquisitive reporters away from her $1.5 million mansion on exclusive Bayshore Boulevard. Kelley claims her honorary counsel status, awarded in April 2012, was the result of her "connections." General Allen, the Commander of the International Security Force for Afghanistan and the designated Supreme Allied Commander of NATO, served in Korea, as did Petraeus. Allen was being investigated for 20,000-30,000 e-mails he allegedly exchanged with Kelley covering a span of time between Allen's stint as the deputy commander of CENTCOM in Tampa in 2010 to the late summer of 2012. There was a great deal of Pentagon spin about the e-mails having no impact on national security. However, the Defense Department Inspector General (IG) narrowed its focus to 60 to 70 e-mails that were said to "bear a fair amount of scrutiny.[28]

The same IG had nabbed General Ward for his misuse of funds while the chief of AFRICOM, while also determining that the NATO commander Allen was due to replace, Admiral James Stavridis, improperly used a military aircraft for himself and his wife to fly to a wine tasters' party in Burgundy in France.[29] In fact, it is rare when flag rank officers are disciplined for misuse of funds, the "military way" being to charge lower-level logistics officers for signing off on the malfeasance. But with the sudden rash of military firings, these were not "normal" military times. Someone at a high level, Panetta, Vice President Joe Biden, or Obama, possibly all three, were kicking some military brass ass. The questions remains, what brought on the series of reprimands?

It has also been revealed that Kelley's twin sister, Natalie Khawam's ex-husband is Grayson Wolfe, who served on the staff of Jerry Bremer's Coalition Provisional Authority in Iraq and was responsible for awarding contracts for the

---

[27] Terry Spencer and Tamara Lush, "Tampa Socialite Fighting Back in Petraeus Scandal," Associated Press, November 27, 2012.
[28] Elisabeth Bumiller and Scott Shane, "Investigation Into General Narrows Look at E-Mail," *New York Times*, November 27, 2012.
[29] *Ibid.*

oil industry and other development projects. Wolfe also worked for the U.S. Export-Import Bank and was a registered lobbyist with the firm Fleischman and Walsh. The firm lobbied the Federal Communications Commission on behalf of the National Cable and Telecommunications Association, Cellular Telecommunications and Internet Association, SBC Communications, AOL, and Verizon. Other clients have included the health care industry, the Electronic Warfare Association (EWA) Information & Infrastructure Technologies, FAA Managers' Association, Continental Airlines, Midway Airlines, Association of American Railroads, Sabre Group (travel industry, airline reservations), Orbitz, TRW Civil Systems, Homeland Security Information Sharing and Analysis Center for the Water Industry, City of Port St. Lucie, Florida, and Cuyahoga County, Ohio.

Wolfe's father is, reportedly, ex-U.S. Army and Special Operations officer Paul G. Wolfe. The elder Wolfe is Program Director for Critical Infrastructure Protection at EWA Information Infrastructure Technologies, Inc. On April 17, 2002, he spoke to a conference, sponsored by the right-wing Lexington Institute at the Longworth House Office Building, on the security threats posed by public interest groups that raised "bogus" health scares about genetically-modified foods and plastic medical body inserts. Joining him on the panel was Senator James Inhofe (R-OK), a member of the Senate Intelligence Committee, as well as spokesmen from the right-wing Hudson Institute and Competitive Enterprise Institute. In 2002, Wolfe joined an "impartial" fact-finding team from the neo-conservative and pro-Israeli Foundation for the Defense of Democracies (FDD), headed by Israeli cipher Clifford May, that traveled to the West Bank to investigate the Israeli Defense Force massacre of Palestinian civilians in Jenin. The FDD team that consisted of the late Congressman Jack Kemp, Representative Brad Sherman (D-CA), and publisher Steve Forbes determined that the UN Relief and Works Agency (UNWRA) and International Red Cross were anti-Semitic and that their reports on the Jenin massacre was biased.

The elder Wolfe also served as the program director for the Department of Homeland Security's Surface Transportation Information Sharing and Analysis Center (ISAC) headquartered in Herndon, Virginia.

Natalie, the attorney who graduated from Georgetown Law School and specialized in protecting whistleblowers, had an acrimonious divorce from and child custody battle with Grayson Wolfe.

Wolfe was also a founding partner of Akkadian Private Ventures, LLC and "affiliated" companies. Akkadia is an extinct empire that existed in what is now Iraq. More interestingly, from January to August 2004, Wolfe worked as the Manager of the Private Sector Development Office of the Coalition Provisional Authority in Baghdad, Iraq and reported to Paul "Jerry" Bremer and his communications director Dan Senor. Wolfe was in Iraq during the same time Petraeus was serving as Commanding General of the 101st Airborne Division. Senor was a chief adviser to Romney in the presidential campaign. Before being assigned to Baghdad, Wolfe was Director of Broader Middle East Initiatives and Iraqi Reconstruction and Special Assistant to the Chief Operating Officer at the Export-Import Bank of the United States at the same time publisher Phil Merrill served the bank as chairman. Merrill, who arranged for the type of loans to Iraq that benefited Wolfe's job of securing contracts for oil and other companies in Iraq and Iraqi Kurdistan, was found in the Chesapeake Bay on June 19, 2006. His feet were wrapped in anchor chain and his body had a bullet wound. The Medical Examiner ruled Merrill's death a suicide.

Akkadian's managing director was oil man and former Bechtel executive Ross Connelly. He served as Maine State Chairman for George W. Bush's presidential campaign. Many of Akkadians' principals are former officials of the Export-Import Bank but the company's website is blocking access to the corporate board of advisers. Akkadian was involved in projects in Pakistan, Egypt, Yemen, and most interestingly, in Libya.

It was also reported that Rhode Island Democratic Party fundraiser Gerald Harrington, founder of the Capitol City Group, Ltd., loaned Khawam $300,000 according to bankruptcy papers filed in April 2012. Moreover, the loan was unsecured. Khawam, according to *The New York Post*, mentioned her connections to Senators John Kerry (D-MA) and Sheldon Whitehouse (D-RI) in her court filings. The *Post* also reported that Harrington may have been engaged to Khawam at some point in time.[30]

Capitol City is a lobbying group that represents the health care industry. Harrington was the National Vice Chairman of Finance for Senator John Kerry's 2004 Presidential campaign. Harrington's Capitol City Group partner,

---

[30] Geoff Earle and Dan Mangan, "Gen. John Allen also helped Jill Kelley's sister during custody battle,"*New York Post*, November 13, 2012.

Christopher Vitale, served on the staff of Representative Patrick Kennedy (D-RI) from 1993 to 1998.

After it was revealed that the North Carolina driver's license of Petraeus's paramour, Paula Broadwell, was found by a jogger in Rock Creek Park in northwest Washington, DC, local DC reporters discovered that Broadwell was staying at the seven-bedroom, $2 million home of her brother, Stephen Kranz, located in the at 1841 Park Road NW, Washington in the Mount Pleasant neighborhood. Kranz bought the home with Carolynn Lafrate, a lawyer who founded Industry Sales Tax Solutions, LLC (ISTS), which bills itself as "a company specializing in providing state and local tax training and publications to a variety of industries including the software and computer services industry." Lafrate previously worked in state and local tax practice for the "Big Four" public accounting firms.

The unidentified jogger turned in the license to the Maryland-National Capital Park Police. There was no information on where the license was found or when it went missing. However, Broadwell's brother's home is in the District of Columbia and the Maryland-National Park Police only have jurisdiction for the Maryland portion of Rock Creek Park, which is part of the National Park Service.

Kranz's home, between 18th and 19th Streets, is virtually around the corner from the 19th and Kenyon location of the home that Prieto shared with another Secret Service agent. Walking west on Park Road on Park, one comes to 19th Street. Walking two blocks, past Lamont and Kilbourne Streets, one arrives at 19th and Kenyon, the scene where Obama's Secret Service agent was found. Prior to being assigned to Obama's detail, Prieto was assigned to the White Plains Secret Service office where he guarded former President Bill Clinton.

Prieto, who was married, was under investigation for an extramarital affair with a Mexican woman. The charges against Prieto stemmed from the scandal involving members of the Secret Service and other White House staff at last April's Summit of the Americas in Cartagena, Colombia.

WMR, which was the first to break the story of Prieto's death, was also told that Washington Metropolitan Police took photographs of homes across the street from the alley location where Prieto's body was discovered in a car. The police crime scene also extended one block west to Kenyon and Adams Mill Road, which adjoins Rock Creek Park where Broadwell's license was found by the jogger. Ironically, Rock Creek Park was where former Representative Gary

Condit's girlfriend Chandra Levy was last thought to have been before she disappeared on May 1, 2001. A year later after an extensive search, Levy's remains were discovered in heavy brush between Broad Branch, Ridge, and Grant Roads in Rock Creek Park.

Prieto's death went officially unreported for several days with the first official news reports dated November 1, 2012. WMR reported the death on October 28 but without the name of the agent that was being withheld by our District of Columbia source.

October 27 was the same day that Cantor said he first heard about Petraeus's affair from Reichert. Reichert heard about the affair from an FBI "source," Humphries, who was in contact with Jill Kelley, the Petraeus friend in Tampa who claimed she was receiving threatening e-mails from Broadwell. Confusing? There's more.

An FBI colleague of Reichert's "source," again Humphries, called Cantor, according to an interview Cantor's Communication director Rory Cooper gave to the Associated Press.[31] That means there were at least two FBI officials who knew about the Petraeus matter presumably before Mueller or Holder knew. It took four full days for Cantor's aide, Sombres, to inform the FBI of the phone call from the FBI personnel who decided to go around their chain-of-command and directly to two very conservative and extremely partisan Republican congressmen in pursuit of what appeared to be political reasons that could affect the fast-approaching November 6 election. This fact is key to the wider conspiracy to prevent Obama's re-election through subterfuge.

The discovery of Broadwell's license in Rock Creek Park was also a mystery. After news of the scandal broke, Broadwell was hiding out at her brother's house near the park.

But why would Broadwell, the most easily-recognized woman in Washington, DC, risk being confronted by the public while jogging in Rock Creek Park? There is the possibility that Broadwell's license was stolen and was placed in the park as a veiled warning for the 40-year old not to talk about details of her affair with Petraeus and her other "connections."

---

[31] Kimberly Dozier, "Petraeus said to be shocked by girlfriends' emails," Associated Press, November 13, 2012.

Broadwell must have been painfully aware of what Rock Creek Park and mistresses meant to everyone in Washington, DC: it is the place where Chandra Levy's remains were discovered a year after she disappeared. The author previously reported that Levy was murdered because she began telling friends what Condit, a member of the House Intelligence Committee, had told her about the upcoming terrorist attack using passenger airplanes on the United States. Condit insisted that Levy not fly back to California but that she should take Amtrak. The discovery of Khawam's in-laws' lobbying connections to America's airline, communications, electronic warfare, and intelligence industries should make Broadwell stop and think what coded messages about Levy's fate and 9/11 were being sent her way. Of course, the Khawam in-laws also had connections to the thousand pound elephant in the 9/11 room: Israel. And that should've focused immediate attention on Cantor, Binyamin Netanyahu's old Boston Consulting Group pal Romney, and other members of Congress who were hoping for a Jimmy Carter-like October Surprise for Obama arising from the Benghazi diplomatic compound attack.

Broadwell's father, Paul Kranz, of Bismarck, North Dakota, stated: "This is about something else entirely, and the truth will come out."[32] Based on the deep connections of L'Affaire Petraeus to America's top intelligence and military echelons, Broadwell's dad appeared to be on to something.

And as for professional women who ply themselves to the rich and powerful, Washington, DC was the scene of an escort service that used highly-intelligence women to bed down politicians, Pentagon brass, and diplomats. After going public with her clients' phone list, Pamela Martin & Associates proprietor Deborah Jeane Palfrey was found hanging in her mother's laundry room in Florida. Levy and Palfrey were two names that were in the minds of many seasoned Washington reporters as the Petraeus scandal unfolded.

---

[32] Laura Collins and Louise Boyle, "'The truth will come out': Father of Petraeus' mistress defends his daughter - as ex-CIA chief 'faces military probe over adultery,'" *Daily Mail*, November 12, 2012.

Chapter 4 – Petraeus's Predecessors and CIA Games

Although Allen Dulles, the early Cold War CIA director, was known as a serial adulterer, it was not until recent years, especially since the end of the Cold War, that the CIA has been plagued with unprofessional and scandalous leadership at the very top.

Ronald Reagan began politicizing the CIA when he brought in New York securities firm executive William Casey to lead the "Agency." Casey, who soon mired the CIA in the Iran-contra scandal that almost brought down Reagan in impeachment, appointed Reagan campaign donor Max Hugel as deputy director for operations. Hugel left amid a cloud of scandal involving his stocks transactions, however, CIA insiders knew that the gruff-talking Hugel, a Brooklyn-born Jew, was fired because of his suspicious contacts with Israeli intelligence officers while he was at the CIA.

President Bill Clinton's first CIA director was lawyer James Woolsey, a Henry "Scoop" Jackson Democrat who had no prior intelligence experience. "Scoop Jackson Democrats," including Richard Perle, Paul Wolfowitz, and I. Lewis "Scooter" Libby were the core of the neo-conservative cabal that emerged inside the George W. Bush administration.

Like Hugel, Woolsey also had close connections with Israeli agents and lobbyists. Woolsey was forced to resign after the exposure of Aldrich Ames, a high-level Soviet agent in the top echelon of the CIA. After he left the CIA, Woolsey became active with the neo-con Project for the New American Century (PNAC), Foundation for the Defense of Democracies, Committee for the Liberation of Iraq, and Center for Security Policy. He became an adviser to John McCain's 2008 presidential campaign against Obama.

John Deutch, a Brussels, Belgium-born Russian Jew, whose background was chemistry and physics, succeeded Woolsey as director. It was discovered that Deutch's unclassified laptop computers contained classified information. However, in what was a worse potential security compromise, classified computers that Deutch took home with him from work were used to access pornographic websites. Security officers were concerned that "cookie" programs used by X-rated websites may have had access to and downloaded classified information from Deutch's laptop. Amid the security flap, Deutch suddenly resigned on December 15, 1996. Clinton pardoned Deutch of any wrongdoing on January 20, 2001 and a Justice Department investigation by Attorney General Janet Reno was put on ice.

George Tenet, a congressional staffer without any prior intelligence experience, succeeded Deutch. It was Tenet who concocted intelligence that Saddam Hussein possessed weapons of mass destruction, telling President Bush on December 12, 2002, that the CIA had a "slam dunk" case against Iraq. Tenet told Bush in June 2004 he wanted to leave for "personal reasons."

Former CIA case officer and House Intelligence Committee chairman Porter Goss became CIA director after Tenet. Goss packed the agency with his own cronies from his congressional staff, infuriating seasoned agency veterans. Goss's executive director Kyle "Dusty" Foggo was later indicted for fraud and Goss's and Foggo's name emerged in connection with the "DC Madam" scandal and poker parties featuring female escorts and heavy drinking at the Watergate Hotel in Washington. Goss resigned suddenly after a meeting with Bush at the White House on May 5, 2006.

Former National Security Agency director General Michael Hayden succeeded Goss. Hayden was criticized for continuing to wear his Air Force uniform at the civilian CIA and Secretary of Defense Robert Gates, himself a former CIA director, instructed Hayden to retire and take off the uniform.

Obama appointed Leon Panetta, a former Democratic Congressman, to succeed Hayden. Panetta's only distinguishing accomplishment at the agency was not getting caught with his pants down or with his hands in some Israeli cookie jar.
WMR has learned from intelligence sources that former CIA director David Petraeus knew during the summer about the plans to discredit President Obama in what failed GOP presidential candidate Mitt Romney called a "Jimmy Carter Strategy" to bring about an October Surprise embassy or diplomatic mission crisis that like Carter, would result in Obama's defeat at the polls.

The Jimmy Carter Strategy included the release of the anti-Muslim "Innocence of Muslims"movie trailer on YouTube that was seen as a catalyst that would trigger an embassy or mission crisis in one or more Arab or Muslim countries. In Benghazi, radical Salafists in the pay of Qatar and Saudi Arabia laid siege to the U.S. compound but, instead of overrunning the compound and taking the ambassador and staff hostage, something went terribly wrong with the plan and Ambassador Christopher Stevens and one Foreign Service officer and two State Department contractors were killed by guerrillas affiliated with "Al Qaeda."

The mere fact that "Al Qaeda" would rear its head again on September 11 was no mistake. The American electorate was being played like a cheap fiddle about the Al Qaeda bogeyman just as it was on October 29, 2004, four days before the November 2 presidential election between President George W. Bush and Democratic Senator John Kerry. A dubious Osama bin Laden video surfaced on Al Jazeera and was transmitted to screens around the world with a warning to the American people. Al Jazeera never disclosed the source of the video. Bush saw his popularity immediately increase and Kerry lost a very close election to Bush. The authenticity of the tape was never proven but bin Laden's rhetorical flourishes benefited Bush:

"Contrary to what [President George W.] Bush says and claims – that we hate freedom –let him tell us then, 'Why did we not attack Sweden?' It is known that those who hate freedom don't have souls with integrity, like the souls of those 19. May the mercy of God be upon them . . . We fought with you because we are free, and we don't put up with transgressions. We want to reclaim our nation. As you spoil our security, we will do so to you . . . I wonder about you. Although we are ushering the fourth year after 9/11, Bush is still exercising confusion and misleading you and not telling you the true reason. Therefore, the motivations are still there for what happened to be repeated . . . We agreed with the leader of the group, Mohammed Atta, to perform all attacks within 20 minutes before Bush and his administration were aware of what was going on. And we never knew that the commander-in-chief of the American armed forces would leave 50,000 of his people in the two towers to face those events by themselves when they were in the most urgent need of their leader. He was more interested in listening to the child's story about the goat rather than worry about what was happening to the towers. So, we had three times the time necessary to accomplish the events. Your security is not in the hands of Kerry or Bush or al Qaeda. Your security is in your own hands."[33]

---

[33] "Bin Laden: Your security is in your own hands," CNN, Octgober 29, 2004.

Bin Laden, or whoever was reading words ascribed to him, issued forth an ultimatum: your security is in your own hands. The ruse worked. Americans would leave their security in the hands of Bush and Dick Cheney for another four years.

It was not merely the anti-Muslim trailer that was designed to create the psychological setting for a 2012 October Surprise. On the evening of September 11, when the U.S. Consulate was being overrun, Petraeus was at a private Washington, DC screening of the movie "Argo," which dramatized the CIA's rescue of six American diplomats from Tehran during the hostage crisis at the U.S. embassy. Ironically, "Argo" was co-produced by Obama fundraiser George Clooney. The movie had extraordinary technical assistance from the CIA, including the agency's Hollywood liaison office in Los Angeles. Part of the filming took place in McLean, Virginia near CIA headquarters. The film has been criticized for a number of historical inaccuracies and screenplay errors, a clue that the movie was put together haphazardly and on a rush schedule.

The Argo operation was a joint CIA-Canadian Security Intelligence Service (CSIS) operation to use a phony Canadian film team, supposedly working on a science fiction movie also called "Argo" and set in Tehran, to spirit six American diplomats from their hiding place at the Canadian ambassador's residence in the Iranian capital. The six Americans were given Canadian passports with fake identities as Canadian filmmakers.

The Wall Street Journal reported that Petraeus's aides were astonished that the director would watch a movie while the Benghazi consulate was under attack.[34] However, if the Benghazi siege had been a hostage situation as planned by the conspirators behind the Jimmy Carter Strategy rather than a massacre of diplomatic personnel, the Argo movie would have reminded the public of the Tehran hostage situation that forced Jimmy Carter from office. The cable news channels, like the nightly ABC News program that spawned "Nightline," would have led each report on the crisis with "day eight of the hostage crisis," "day nine," and so forth, until Election Day. "Argo" concludes with Jimmy Carter's speech about the hostages after they were released just as Ronald Reagan was being sworn in as president on January 20, 1981.

---

[34] Greta van Susteren, "Report: Petraeus saw 'Argo' during Benghazi attack," *The Washington Times*, November 2, 2012.

On October 10, Petraeus and his wife Holly attended an invitation-only screening of "Argo" at the Canadian embassy. The screening was also attended by Hillary Clinton aide Huma Abedin and her husband, former Representative Anthony Weiner (D-NY), who resigned after he tweeted photos of his genitals to women he didn't personally know. Abedin, a native of Michigan, lived for some time in Jeddah, Saudi Arabia. A few Republicans in Congress charged that Abedin had ties with the Muslim Brotherhood, allegations that were strongly rejected by two of Obama's chief critics over the deadly Benghazi compound raid, Senators John McCain (R-AZ) and Lindsey Graham (R-SC).

Petraeus was said to have been out of sorts during the Canadian embassy screening and reception. Many people close to Petraeus commented that he had become increasingly detached from his CIA responsibilities after he became aware of the investigation of so-called threatening e-mails sent by his mistress Paula Broadwell to Tampa socialite Jill Kelley. It has also been discovered that Kelley hosted several social functions for Republican National Convention Romney delegates and convention guests during the last week of August.

There are reports that Petraeus had confided to a select few of his friends that he was planning on leaving the CIA after the November 6 election and wanted to take over as the president of Princeton University. Broadwell's Wikipedia page contained an entry from January of this year, one that was subsequently deleted, that states: "Petraeus is reportedly one of her many conquests." The notation by an anonymous editor indicates that Petraeus was not the only target for Broadwell's affection and may be the indication that Broadwell served as a "honey trap" for a wider intelligence operation. The June 11, 2012 photo of Broadwell with GOP master operative Karl Rove opens all sorts of possibilities into the Broadwell-as-a-Mata Hari scenario. There is also the question of the role of Jill Kelley and her sister Natalie Khawam in the "aggressive housewife" net that had also ensnared the commander of the International Security Assistance Force-Afghanistan and NATO commander-designate General John Allen and former Central Command chief John Abizaid, who, like the Jill and Natalie twins, is of Lebanese descent.

The relational pentagon between Generals Petraeus and Allen, Army Reserve Lt. Col., biographer, and faux journalist Paula Broadwell, and Lebanese-American twins Jill Kelley and Natalie Khawam has all the makings of a honeypot operation involving one or more intelligence agencies. That was the conclusion of senior Pentagon and CIA officials who insisted on anonymity. It is noteworthy that Allen's official biography states that official biography states that he is "the first Marine Corps officer inducted as a Term Member of the Council on Foreign Relations."

Petraeus and Allen were soon the subject of a multitude of national security investigations by the FBI. The CIA, and the Department of Defense, including the Pentagon's Inspector General and the Defense Intelligence Agency. The FBI also investigated its Tampa special agent, Humphries, who, beyond sending a bizarre shirtless photograph of himself to Tampa socialite Kelley, was under investigation for unofficial contacts with GOP Representatives Reichert and Eric about Petraeus's affair with Broadwell. Humphries, who is bald, sent a photo of himself to Kelley while conducting SWAT training at MacDill Air Force base and posing with two bald dummies.

Kelley was designated as a socialite liaison between the State Department's International Visitor Leadership Program (IVLP) and MacDill Air Force Base, which hosts as tenant commands CENTCOM, where Petraeus and Lebanese-American General John Abizaid served as commanders, and USSOCOM, which oversees the activities of the Navy SEALS and the Army Green Berets. The IVLP maintains over 90 "international councils" around the United States that facilitate the visits of foreign aspiring leaders to the United States for "cultural and educational" exchange purposes. In fact, CIA files indicate that such cultural and educational exchange programs have long been used by U.S. intelligence to develop long-term contacts with foreigners thought to be on the fast track for Senior leadership positions in their countries.

When the IVLP program began in 1948 and was merged with the "Foreign Leaders Program," it immediately set about to link foreign leaders with senior U.S. military officers and intelligence officials. The Cold War influence peddling to counter-act Soviet propaganda was the goal of the programs two chief sponsors in the U.S. Senate, the extreme right-wing H. Alexander Smith (R-NJ) and Karl Mundt (R-SD). The Smith-Mundt Act of 1948, known as the Information and Educational Exchange Act, created the basis for current IVLP program, which was used by Kelley to introduce senior foreign military officers assigned to training and liaison positions at MacDill to U.S. generals and admirals. Kelley apparently had little time for any American officer under the rank of colonel.

As honorary consul for South Korea, Kelley reportedly tried to arrange for finder's fees for contracts worth in the millions of dollars by claiming she could successfully connect well-heeled Republican donors attending the Republican National Convention in Tampa with South Korean business ventures. South Korea was embarrassed when Kelley tried to use her honorific status to claim that her mansion home on Bayshore Boulevard in Tampa had diplomatic immunity from curious reporters and news photographers. South Korea's government eventually relieved Kelley of her honorary consul status after conducting a review of the situation. South Korea is known to have maintained an active and somewhat aggressive intelligence-gathering and influence-peddling operation in the United States that involved the former Korean Central Intelligence Agency and a Washington intermediary named Tongsun Park. Park was a Washington, DC socialite, nicknamed the "Asian Great Gatsby," who was indicted in 1977 for bribing members of Congress on behalf of interests that wanted to maintain U.S. troop levels in South Korea. The scandal tarnished House Speaker Carl Albert who declined to run for re-election.

South Korea's presidential decree number 23706 granted Kelley the duties of "working to protect Korean nationals/residents living abroad" and "promoting interacting of trade, economy, art, science, and education."

USA Today reported that in 2010, Kelley sky-dived with commandos from SOCOM. The paper also reported that French and Italian officers were particularly fond of Kelley's grand social mixers held at her Tampa home, where foreign and U.S. officers mingled with Tampa politicians and businessmen.[35] It should be noted that Park's Georgetown Club on Wisconsin Avenue in the tony Washington neighborhood was used for similar purposes.

Petraeus once arrived at one of Kelley's parties with a 28-police car motorcade from MacDill, which is only 6 miles from Kelley's home.

---

[35] Tom Vanden Brook Donna Leinwand Leger and Michael Winter, "Socialite Jill Kelley Skydived with Commandos," *USA Today*, November 16, 2012.

PHOTO: WMR staff. WMR and all of Tampa's TV and newspaper media staked out the 1005 Bayshore Boulevard mansion of Jill Kelley. On November 15, the only afternoon activity was the Kelleys' nanny returning with the two children from Publix, where she had been grocery shopping.

The IVLP program may have played a role in establishing the necessary contacts for the United States to gain diplomatic support in the Caribbean for the 1983 invasion of Grenada. A number of Caribbean leaders that came to the Reagan administration's side during the invasion were past participants of the IVLP, including Grenada Governor General Paul Scoon, Barbados Prime Minister Tom Adams, Dominica Prime Minister Eugenia Charles, and Nevis Prime Minister Simeon Daniel.

Other IVLP participants include such pro-U.S. leaders as Australian Prime Minster Julia Gillard, Philippines President Glorida-Macapagal Arroyo, former Danish Prime Minister and current NATO Secretary General Anders Fogh Rasmussen, former French President Nicolas Sarkozy, Indian Prime Minister Manmohan Singh, Georgian President Mikheil Saakashvili, Afghan President Hamid Karzai, convicted former Icelandic Prime Minister Geir Haarde, former Norwegian Prime Minister Kjell Magne Bondevik, former British Prime Ministers Tony Blair and Gordon Brown, former British Prime Minister Edward Heath (implicated in the BBC pedophile scandal surrounding television celebrity Jimmy Savile), Cook Islands Prime Minister Terepai Tuamure Maoate, imprisoned for rape former Israeli President Moshe Katsav, Qatar Prime Minister Hamad bin Jassim bin Jaber Al Thani, and former Venezuelan President Rafael Caldera.

Karl Rove's political client and friend, Swedish Prime Minister Fredrik Reinfeldt, is also a past participant of the IVLP.

PHOTO: WMR staff. Jill Kelley's Mercedes with Florida honorary consul tags.

Most interestingly, South Korea has the lion's share of past participants in the IVLP: Presidents Kim Dae-jung and Kim Young-sam, and Prime Ministers Han Seung-soo, Hyun Seung-jong, Lee Yung-duk, Kim Sang-hyup, Nam Duck-woo, Chun Il-kwon, Lee Han-key, and Choi Doo-sun.

On Thursday afternoon, November 8, former CIA director Porter Goss, who resigned amid his own scandal involving Watergate poker parties and female escorts working for the late Deborah Jeane Palfrey, arrived at Langley with other past CIA directors to discuss an issue "unrelated to Benghazi." Goss would not state why the past CIA directors were at Langley to see Petraeus, however, they were told that Petraeus was not at CIA headquarters but across the Potomac at the White House. While a group of past CIA directors were at Langley ready to talk to Petraeus about an undisclosed topic, Petraeus was tendering his resignation to President Obama over his affair with Broadwell. Goss splits his time between Washington, DC and Sanibel, Florida. Dr. Russell Broadwell, the father of Broadwell's husband, Dr. Scott Broadwell, also lives on Sanibel island, south of Tampa, but he's not talking to the media and chased away a WINK-TV news crew away from his door. Dr. Russell Broadwell and

Goss live a few blocks from one another in the tony Sanibel 33957 zip code, where homes average $850,000.

Chapter 5 – Karl Rove, again!

CIA sources, speaking on deep background, told WMR that Humphries, the FBI agent who allegedly took it upon himself to contact Representatives Reichert and inform him, and ultimately Representative Cantor, the House Majority Leader, about Petraeus's affair with biographer Paula Broadwell, may have been working with GOP strategist Karl Rove.

Rove has long been rumored to have close links to certain CIA operations, including those in Sweden. Rove has been a political adviser to Swedish Prime Minister Fredrik Reinfeldt, a conservative who has sidled up to the CIA on issues ranging from the CIA's rendition of Muslims from Swedish soil, CIA use of Swedish airfields for rendition activity, and the attempt by the United States to bring WikiLeaks founder Julian Assange to face trial in the United States.

The Broadwell connection to Rove is key. The death list of those with a possible connection to the Petraeus scandal does not end with Ivens, Prieto, Stevens, and the other Benghazi personnel. On November 9, mere hours before the Petraeus resignation was reported, the body of a private security guard for Reinfeldt was discovered at the Prime Minister's waterfront Sagerska Palace in Stockholm. The guard, said to be a "familiar face" around the palace, worked for *Svensk BevakningsTjänst*, Sweden's third largest security company, which is owned by the large conglomerate Axel Johnson AB. Renfeldt and his family were not home at the time of the death, which was said to have been caused by an "accidental" or "self-inflicted" gun shot. Is there a connection between the suspicious death of the private guard for Rove's friend Reinfeldt and Obama's Secret Service agent and the FBI agent in Los Angeles? Did one or more of them know too much?

Broadwell with Karl Rove, June 11, 2012.

Obama never allowed himself to be drawn into the trap laid for him over Benghazi by Romney, Rove, disloyal military officers, and some CIA elements. There are indications the conspiracy against Obama was large. The same day that Petraeus resigned, officially over an "extramarital affair," Christopher Kubisek, the incoming CEO of America's largest defense contractor, Lockeed Martin, was fired by the company's board for a "close, personal relationship" with a subordinate.

If such a series of resignations and forced retirements were to occur in other countries, the CIA would call them a government purge. Former CIA officer Robert Baer said in an interview that he knew of past CIA directors who had extramarital affairs but the FBI had never been called in to investigate.

Baer told CNN's Piers Morgan on November 9, 2012:

> "There are 4 or 5 CIA directors that I know who were carrying on extramarital affairs while they were director. The FBI was never brought in . . . So this is absolutely extraordinary. I'm telling you there's more to do than with sex. There's something going on here which I can't explain and I think we're going to find out very soon."[36]

---

[36] CNN, November 9, 2012, Piers Morgan Tonight, "Robert Baer on the FBI investigation into the extramarital affair that caused the resignation of CIA Director David Petraeus."

The FBI was never called in to investigate the many alleged affairs of CIA director Allen W. Dulles, even though FBI director J. Edgar Hoover had an obsessive interest in the sexual activities of others, or the more recent reported affairs of CIA director Michael Hayden while he was NSA director. Baer may have been referring to Hayden, as well as Dulles in his count.

The author was told that Rove continues to maintain close contacts with the FBI, links he established years ago while he worked in Austin, Texas. In 1986, while working on the campaign of Republican gubernatorial candidate Bill Clements, Rove declared publicly that Clements' opponent's campaign had bugged his office. Rove had falsely accused the campaign of incumbent Democratic Governor Mark White of placing the bug in Rove' office. In 1973, Rove was interviewed by an FBI agent on suspicions that Rove had engaged in dirty tricks during Watergate, including rummaging through his opponent's trash cans during his run for the presidency of the College Republicans. No charges were ever filed against Rove.

Rove's office bug was placed with the assistance of FBI agent Greg Rampton, a Rove friend. Later, in 1990, Rampton was used to tarnish Agriculture Commissioner candidate Jim Hightower, who was running against Rove's candidate Rick Perry. As of 2007, Rampton denied any "intelligence" relationship with Rove but defended him from charges that he engaged in dirty tricks. Rampton was later one of the lead FBI agents at the 1992 siege of Randy Weaver's compound in Ruby Ridge, Idaho.

In 1991, the Texas Senate held confirmation hearings for Rove to serve on the East Texas State University Board of Regents. Rove was questioned by Senator Bob Glasgow on Rampton and the 1986 gubernatorial campaign.

> **Glasgow:** Ah, Mr. Rove, would you now tell us publicly who bugged your office that you blamed upon Mark White publicly and the press statewide?
>
> **Rove:** Ah, first of all, I did not blame it on Mark White. If, ah, if you'll recall I specifically said at the time that we disclosed the bugging that we did not know who did it, but we knew who might benefit from it. And no, I do not know. ...
>
> **Glasgow:** And are you now satisfied that Mark White and the Democratic Party did not bug your office as you . . . as you released, ah, to the newspapers?

Rove: Senator, I never said Mark White bugged my office, I'm not certain he has an electronic background. I never said the Democratic Party bugged it either. ... As to who bugged it, Senator, I do not know ... and the FBI does not know. ...

Glasgow: How long have you known an FBI agent by the name of Greg (Rampton)?

Rove: Ah, Senator, it depends, would you define "know" for me?

Glasgow: What is your relationship with him?

Rove: Ah, I know, I would not recognize Greg (Rampton) if he walked in the door. We have talked on the phone a var – a number of times. Ah, and he has visited in my office once or twice, but we do not have a social or personal relationship whatsoever. ...

Glasgow: During the Rick Perry campaign (against Jim Hightower), did you have any conversations with FBI agent Rampton about the course and conduct of that campaign?

Rove: Yes, I did, two or three times. ...

Glasgow: Did you issue a press release in Washington, at a fund-raiser, about information you'd received from the FBI implicating – implicating, ah, Hightower?

Rove: We did not issue a press release. ... We did not issue a news release. I talked to a member of the press ...

Glasgow: I'm gonna let you expound on anything you want to. Ah, involved in campaigns that you've been involved in, do you know why agent Rampton conducted a criminal investigation of Garry Mauro at the time you were involved in that campaign, pulled the finance records of Bob Bullock at the time you were involved in that campaign, pulled the campaign records of Jim Hightower at the time you were involved in that campaign?

Rove: Well, Senator, first of all, as I said before, I was not involved in either Bob Bullock or Garry Mauro's campaigns or the campaigns of their Republican opponent. I'd be hard pressed to tell you who Garry Mauro's opponent was in 1986. Ah, and I'd think I'd be hard pressed even to remember who Bob Bullock's opponent was in 1986. So I can't answer that part of the question. I do know that I became involved in Rick Perry's campaign in November of 1989. At that point there was already an investigation ongoing of the Texas Department of Agriculture, prompted by stories which had appeared in August and September, I believe, in *The Dallas Morning News* regarding the use of Texas Department of Agriculture funds.

There is reason for some in the CIA to believe that Rove has a similar relationship with Humphries, the "obsessive" FBI agent who sent shirtless photographs of himself to Tampa socialite Jill Kelley. Humphries supervised the Joint Terrorism Task Force in Tampa and he enjoyed unfettered access to MacDill Air Force Base, including the U.S. Special Operations Command.

In 2011, Petraeus also awarded Kelley with the Joint Chiefs of Staff Award for Outstanding Public Service. The award is the second-highest honor that the Joint Chiefs can award a civilian. The award was approved by the then-Joint Chiefs of Staff chairman Admiral Mike Mullen. The citation read, in part, that Kelley received the award for her "willingness to host engagements with Senior National Representatives from more than 60 countries was indicative of her support for both the Coalition's effort and the mission of United States Central Command."[37]

Colonel Col. E.J Otero, the founder of CENTCOM's Coalition Intelligence Center, the element that coordinates the visit of high-ranking foreign officials to MacDill, stated that Kelley was an important figure at MacDill, telling Fox News 13 in Tampa, "When a senior national representative from the coalition had a visitor from another country coming into town, they would call her – 'I have General such-and-such. Do you mind if we go and have dinner?'"[38]

It was reported that Kelley made three trips with her family to the White House, one as late as November 4, two days before the election and six days after Cantor notified the FBI about Petraeus's affair with Broadwell.[39] The other two visits were on October 24 when Jill and Natalie had lunch at the White House Mess and a breakfast meeting between Jill and Natalie on September 24.[40]

---

[37] Howard Altman, "Kelley awarded Joint Chiefs No. 2 medal for civilians," *The Tampa Tribune*, November 21, 2012.
[38] Gloria Gomez, "Jill Kelley's role at MacDill,"Fox News 13 Tampa, November 21, 2012.
[39] Amy Gardner, "Jill Kelley, twin sister visited White House three times in autumn of 2012," *Washington Post*, November 16, 2012.
[40] William R. Levesque and Alex Leary, "Jill Kelley's world: White House visits, meals with generals, and name-dropping emails to Tampa mayor," *Tampa Bay Times*, November 17, 2012.

On June 11, 2012, Broadwell and Rove were photographed together in Washington, DC at a conference of state legislators. A month after seeing Rove in Washington, Broadwell was in Aspen where she let it be known that she had been approached by the Republican Party to run for the U.S. Senate in 2014 against incumbent Democrat Kay Hagan. Broadwell said Petraeus was "irritated" at the notion of a Senate run and shot the idea down.[41]

Kelley was said to have met with a "mid-level" White House staffer on all three occasions. The staffer was reported to have previously worked as a civilian lawyer for the U.S. military in Afghanistan and met Kelley on a trip to MacDill. The staffer was also reported to have been a lawyer in the White House on Obama's staff.[42] The U.S. Secret Service stated that the name of the staffer would be revealed when the White House visitor logs were released. At the time of publication of this book, the logs had not been released.

Gary Welsh of the website Advanceindiana.blogspot.com contacted the author and offered the most likely explanation for the identity of the White House attorney who was Kelley's and Khawam's interlocutor, Michael J. Gottlieb, a special assistant and associate counsel to the President.

Gottlieb, from January 2010 to March 2011 was assigned to to Kabul as the Deputy Director of Combined Joint Interagency Task Force 435, which was responsible for military detention operations . What is more interesting is that Gottlieb's time in Afghanistan overlapped with Petraeus's command from July 4, 2010, to July 18, 2011, which means that one of Obama's lawyers would have known Petraeus and certainly have been in on the rumors about the relationship between the general and his frequent visitor and biographer, Paula Broadwell. Welsh posed an interesting question: How could Obama have said he first found out about Petraeus's affair on November 7, when one of Obama's own White House attorneys, someone who had met Kelley and her sister three times in the weeks and days before the election, would have certainly been privy to it while in Afghanistan? Either Gottlieb told the president early on or he sat on it for other reasons. [43]

In any event, Jill and Natalie soon became "lawyered up," Washington-speak for having their access to the press curtailed and highly vetted. Jill had Abbe Lowell as her attorney while Natalie retained celebrity lawyer Gloria

---

[41] Tim Funk, "Paula Broadwell, U.S. senator?" *Charlotte Observer*, November 17, 2012.
[42] Levesque and Leary, op. cit.

[43] Gary Welsh, "The White House Attorney Who Knew Jill Kelley: Michael J. Gottlieb?" http://advanceindiana.blogspot.com/2012/11/the-white-house-attorney-who-knew-jill.html November 19, 2012.

Allred. Paula also hired her own "protection" in Glover Park Group, owned by the world's largest advertising firm, WPP Plc., and having on its staff the former press secretary for President Clinton, Dee Dee Myers. Petraeus also decided to hire on as his attorneys the long-time CIA-connected Williams & Connolly.

Kelley had an unofficial position at MacDill that many intelligence professionals have called unusual for a high-security base. Kelley and General Allen reportedly exchanged some 30,000 emails with one another. That is also unusual, especially for a wartime commander. Kelley was also on a first name basis with Petraeus and hosted him and his wife at her Tampa mansion for lavish receptions for the U.S. and foreign military brass stationed at MacDill Air Force Base.

Broadwell also reportedly visited the White House on two occasions. However, it is not known who she was visiting and who authorized her visit.

PHOTO: WMR. Jill Kelley's Bayshore Boulevard mansion. Kelley bragged to Tampa Democratic Mayor Bob Buckhorn *about her visit to the White House, stating she was glad "POTUS" was re-elected. Kelley started a Tampa firestorm when she threatened to sue Tampa shock-jock "Bubba The Love Sponge," aka* Todd Clem, *for threatening to "deep fry" a Koran. Buckhorn called the DJ a moron over the controversy about the Koran. "Bubba" has threatened to subject Buckhorn to shock jock-style retaliation. Clem has been a habitué of professional wrestling and Howard Stern-on-demand TV programs. For the Tampa portion of the Petraeus saga, Clem became a convenient diversion for certain parties, including those long-affiliated with his former syndicator, the conservative Republican Clear Channel.*

PHOTOS: WMR. TV trucks parked outside Kelley's Tampa home. The Tampa media will jump at anything salacious in their coverage of Kelley. One TV reporter was informed about the dead presidential detail Secret Service agent found around the corner from Broadwell's brother's residence in Washington, DC. He shrugged his shoulders, saying, "I didn't hear about that."

There is an interesting aside to the Petraeus scandal that was largely ignored by the media. Petraeus was a common denominator in the fall from command of two of his immediate predecessors as a result of impertinent remarks they made about their respective commanders-in-chief. George W. Bush and Barack Obama. WMR reported on this unusual twist on July 9, 2010:

July 9-11, 2010 – Did McChrystal fire himself?

WMR has learned from U.S. intelligence sources that General Stanley McChrystal, the former commander of the International Security Assistance Force for Afghanistan and the Commander of U.S. Forces in Afghanistan, fired by President Obama for impertinent remarks about Obama, Vice President Joseph Biden, National Security Adviser James

Jones, and U.S. Special Envoy to Afghanistan Richard Holbrooke made to a *Rolling Stone* reporter, knew exactly what he was doing when he criticized his senior chain-of-command.

The article, titled "The Runaway General," was exactly on the mark with the "runaway general" implication in the title. Like McChrystal, former US Central Command commander, Admiral William Fallon was fired after an interview was published in *Esquire* magazine stating that he opposed the Bush administration's plans to attack Iran and that he was the only person standing in the way of such action. Defense Secretary Robert Gates forced Fallon to resign and retire, just as he did with McChystal. McChrystal is also known to have opposed a U.S. military attack on Iran.

Seeing that Fallon got out from under a disastrous policy by giving an interview to *Esquirer*, McChrystal and his staff gave the green light for the *Rolling Stone* interview, knowing what the ultimate outcome would be. Fallon was asked to resign as CENTCOM commander for disagreeing with George Bush, McChrystal was shown the door by disagreeing openly with Barack Obama. And, in an ironic situation, both Fallon and McChrystal were replaced by General David Petraeus, the neocons' favorite general.

Petraeus is an arm chair general who has spent more time in neocon think tanks being politically indoctrinated on U.S. global control than on the battlefield with the war fighters.

In March 2007, according to IPS News, Fallon called Petraeus, his Iraq commander, "an ass kissing little chicken shit" to his face, adding, "I hate people like that," The *Esquire* interview came in December 2007, with the interview appearing in March 2008. Whether it was Fallon calling Petraeus a "chicken shit" or McChrystal calling Jones a "clown," the results were the same: both were forced to retire and it was Gates who wielded the mighty Pentagon ax.

Gates, the personal overseer for the Bush family, and Petraeus, the neocon armchair general, have been the common denominators in both the Fallon and McChrystal self-purges. For the military, the problems are neither Fallon or McChrystal, but the global extenders of U.S. military power – Gates and Petraeus.

The next flag rank officer to fall on his sword may be Joint Chiefs of Staff Chairman Michael Mullen, who is also known to be opposed to any military attack on Iran. Although he has been careful to make nice publicly with the Israelis, Mullen told the Israeli military leadership in July 2008 not to launch a "USS Liberty Part II" to provoke a US-led war against Iran. The Israelis attacked the US Navy intelligence collection ship, USS Liberty, during the 1967 Six Day War in what some believe was a "false flag" attack designed to pin the blame for the attack on Egypt. After that ploy failed, Israel and its supporters in the Lyndon Johnson administration launched a major cover-up, one that exists to this day.

Chapter 6 – Benghazi: A foreign "false flag" attack?

The party or parties responsible for the September 11, 2012, attack on the U.S. mission in Benghazi, Libya may have a history of such attacks aimed at American targets in the Middle East. Amid the controversy between members of Congress and the Obama administration over the cause for the attack on the mission that killed U.S. ambassador to Libya Stevens and three other State Department personnel, one obscure previously classified CIA report may hold the key.

The Benghazi controversy centers on whether the attack resulted from a spontaneous protest caused by the YouTube posting of an anti-Muslim video titled "The Innocence of Muslims -- the talking point put forth by U.S. ambassador to the UN Susan Rice -- or the attack was well-planned in advance by Libyan terrorists. Both answers may be correct, with the video merely serving as both a catalyst and diversion to mask those actually behind the attack.

From the start of the anti-American demonstrations that swept the Middle East and Muslim world and could have resulted in the storming and occupation of a number of U.S. embassies in the region, from Cairo to Jakarta – thus resulting in Mitt Romney's "Jimmy Carter Strategy" to unseat President Obama -- there were Israeli fingerprints. A number of producers of the video trailer were identified as Los Angeles area Jews who may have been using Egyptian Copts as cover.

The attack on the Benghazi mission, which may have been planned to be a kidnapping by Libyan rebels, thus providing the Romney campaign with its "October Surprise," did not go as planned. The U.S. presence in Benghazi was under the control not of the State Department but the CIA and the Defense Department, rife with Romney supporters among the flag ranks, was kept out of the loop for any rescue mission of the trapped U.S. diplomats. It is also known that Petraeus's mistress, Broadwell, a potential Republican candidate for the U.S. Senate from North Carolina, was privy to classified information concerning the

U.S. diplomatic mission in Benghazi, including CIA detainee operations involving certain Libyan militants.

A formerly SECRET CIA report, titled "Terrorism Review" and issued by the CIA's Directorate of Intelligence on August 9, 1984, paints a similar story of Israelis trying to stoke anti-American violence in the Arab world.

In 1984, long before the advent of the Internet and YouTube, Israeli provocateurs used the mail to fan the flames of violence against U.S. diplomatic targets in the Middle East.

The CIA reported that on July 18, 1984, "U.S. diplomatic installations in Tunis, Sanaa, and Jidda received threatening letters postmarked in Tunis allegedly written by the Arab Revolutionary Brigades (ARB)." [See page 119] The ARB was part of the Abu Nidal Organization but it was later reported by Robert Fisk in the October 25, 2008, *Independent* of the UK that that Abu Nidal was a CIA agent and also served as an agent for Mossad.[44]

The letters sent to U.S. missions from Tunis were attempting to place U.S. diplomat in danger by claiming "Mossad agents posing as U.S. citizens operate out of U.S. diplomatic missions against Arab interests."

The group claiming to be ARB said that their group would "take action" unless the U.S. diplomats were expelled. The CIA reported that the Tunisian authorities intercepted 20 more letters addressed to various U.S. embassies in the Middle East.

The CIA concluded that although the name Arab Revolutionary Brigades had been used by "elements of the Abu Nidal Group," the group "has not sent unauthenticated warnings before conducting past operations and generally has avoided attacking U.S. targets."

Just as the CIA report begins delving into the "disturbing new departure" for the group and that the threat potential was determined to be "extremely low," the remainder of the report is heavily redacted, common when the threats to the United States by Mossad are concerned. In the CIA, as well as the FBI, National Security Agency, and Defense Intelligence Agency, the mere suggestion that Israel could pose a security threat to the United States is often a "career killer." 1984 was a particularly testy time for U.S.-Israeli relations after the

---

[44] Robert Fisk, "Abu Nidal, notorious Palestinian mercenary, 'was a US spy,'" *The Independent*, October 25, 2008.

bombing the previous year of the U.S. Marine Barracks in Beirut. It was reported that Israel withheld critical intelligence from the United States that could have prevented the bombing and saved the lives of 241 American servicemen.

In the January 13, 2012, *Foreign Policy*, Mark Perry reported on Mossad agents running Jundallah Baluchi guerrillas in 2007 and 2008 in Pakistan by falsely claiming they were CIA agents, not Israelis. The Mossad tasked the Jundallah guerrillas to carry out terrorist attacks in Iran. When the CIA discovered that the Mossad was claiming to be CIA in their recruitment of Baluchi Pakistani terrorists, the CIA reported the Israeli operation to the White House. Several reports emanated from the region that stated that the CIA was backing Jundallah but the CIA claimed its policy was to avoid such support. The CIA then discovered that it was Mossad that was providing backing to the terrorists by claiming to be CIA. President Bush reportedly "went ballistic" over the Israeli operation because of the effect it had on fragile U.S.-Pakistan relations and because it put every American at risk.[45]

Petraeus was no stranger to permitting willful terrorist attacks while he commanded U.S. forces in Iraq. Just as Petraeus could have saved the lives of the four Americans in Benghazi in 2012, he could have also saved the lives of countless Americans and Iraqis had he not rendered support to the Shi'a Mahdi Army in Iraq.

On April 14, 2009, WMR ran the following story on Petraeus's support for terrorist actions in Iraq:

> April 14, 2009 – EXCLUSIVE SPECIAL REPORT. Americans and Iraqis died while U.S. took no action against identified Mahdi Army bomb cell
>
> WMR has learned from a private military contractor source who, in 2007, worked at Tallil Air Base in Iraq, that he was given a list of members of a bomb detonation cell working within Muqtada al Sadr's Shi'a militia, the Mahdi Army or "Jaish al Mahdi," but no action was taken by the U.S. military. The inaction by senior US military officers and US intelligence and law enforcement agencies cost the lives of a number of U.S. military service personnel and Iraqi civilians.
>
> On April 8, 2009, WMR reported: "WMR has been informed by a former private military contractor in Iraq that the United States was aware of the identities and even the cell phone numbers of several bomb making operatives within Muqtada al Sadr's Mahdi Army. The bomb cells were

---

[45] Mark Perry, "False Flag," *Foreign Policy*, January 13, 2012.

responsible for detonating a number of bombs in Iraq that targeted Sunnis and coalition personnel, including Americans."

WMR has obtained the list of Mahdi Army bomb cell operatives who targeted U.S. troops and Iraqi civilians. The unit worked closely with Iranian intelligence agents active in Iran. Iran's government denied, at the time, any connection to the bombing attacks in Iraq. The CIA, FBI, and U.S. military intelligence and criminal investigators failed to act against the bomb cell because they were ordered by senior officers in the military chain-of-command, including General David Petraeus, the then-Commanding General of the Multi-National Force-Iraq (MNF-I), and his predecessor, General George Casey, later promoted to Army Chief of Staff, not to put in jeopardy a six month extension of a cease-fire agreement agreed to by the MNF-I and al Sadr's Shi'a militia in 2006. The US ambassador to Iraq, Ryan Crocker, also participated in the conspiracy to avoid taking down the Mahdi Army bomb cell, according to WMR's sources.

In February 2007, the first Petraeus "surge" troops began arriving in Iraq. During 2006, the Mahdi Army was on a virtual bombing spree aimed at Sunnis and foreign forces in Iraq. In 2007, in cooperation with the U.S. "surge," al Sadr agreed to a cease fire in his civil war against the Sunnis of Iraq but his bomb cell, known to US military commanders, was permitted to operate freely. Although a list of some of the bombers was provided to Petraeus and his command, he took no action to bring those who committed acts of terror against U.S. and coalition forces to justice. Petraeus changed the subject by blaming terrorist acts in Iraq on "Al Qaeda."

The Mahdi Army bomb cell list had been passed to a coalition intermediary from a friendly Iraqi asset at great risk to the safety of the asset and his family. Because of the sensitivity of the list, only extracts gleaned from it follow. The list was provided to the U.S. Army's Criminal Investigative Division (CID) at Tallil Air Base in 2007, but no action was taken. In fact, the list was called bogus by military and CIA personnel. The partial publication of the information found in the list reflects an editorial decision by WMR to protect the source of the list and the source's potential contacts inside the Mahdi Army and Iranian intelligence who volunteered the information:

- the arms supply network for the Mahdi Army originated in Maraghen, Iran and terminated in the Karrada district of Baghdad.

- Mahdi Army officers placed orders for weapons and bomb making supplies in Karrada and these were sent to Maraghen to be filled by Iranian intelligence intermediaries.

- A father and son team in Jaderiya, Baghdad was responsible for bomb making and arranging the planting of devices. This team of Akiel Salam Hamid, nicknamed "Al Iranie," and his kingpin father, Hussein Salim Hamid, was tasked with counting military vehicles in the area of Jaderiya and selected targets and build roadside improvised explosive devices (IEDs) consisting mainly of Semtex. Their mobile number, 07702 668 185, and Iraqi government-issued land line number, 7786495, the former of which could have been of great use to National Security Agency (NSA) signals intelligence analysts to determine the team's locations and plans, was apparently never utilized as "actionable intelligence."

The Jaderiya father-son team made the bomb that exploded outside the Fiqma ice cream shop in Karrada on August 1, 2007. Some two dozen Iraqi civilians were killed. Three U.S. soldiers were killed the same day by a roadside bomb in Baghdad. They were Army Staff Sgt. Fernando Santos, 29, San Antonio; Army Spc. Cristian Rojas-Gallego, 24, Loganville, Georgia.; and Army Spc. Eric D. Salinas, 25, Houston. The three were assigned to the 2nd Battalion, 3rd Infantry Regiment, 3rd Brigade, 2nd Infantry Division, Fort Lewis, Washington. The number of US troops killed by Mahdi bomb cell IED explosions could number in the hundreds but the Pentagon is keeping many of the details on these attacks and their victims classified. WMR can report that officers of the U.S. Air Force at Tallil Air Base, as well as US Army officers and criminal investigators at the Department of Defense, were informed about the Mahdi Army bomb cell but no action was taken. WMR is prepared to release the names of those officers and agents who were provided the information about the bomb cell if we are not provided with answers to questions about why no action was taken to protect American troops and Iraqi civilians from the Shi'a militia bombing attacks.

That attack was blamed by U.S. military commanders on Iran but the same commanders had failed to eliminate the bomb making cell when provided with critical intelligence on its composition and methods of operation. The multiple August 1, 2007 bombings in Baghdad that killed over 70 people caused the Sunni Accordance Front bloc, including Deputy Prime Minister Salam al-Zobaie, to quit the Shi'a-dominated Iraqi cabinet of Prime Minister Nouri al-Maliki.

US military authorities were also provided with the mobile numbers of two assassins working for Hussein Salim Hamid, 079022 72814 and 07902272814. The latter was used by a top Mahdi Army coordinator of bombings and assassinations targeting U.S. military personnel and Iraqi civilians.

WMR has also learned of a secret and steady shipment of mortars by U.S. forces into Iraq. The shipment of mortars created a feud between MNF-I commander, General Casey, and Iraqi President Jalal Talabani. Talabani was furious when he learned that the U.S. was shipping mortars into Iraq at the same time the Iraqi government was trying to destroy its own stockpile. On August 31, 2005, mortar fire directed at Shi'a pilgrims allegedly by "Al Qaeda" leader Abu Musab al Zarqawi, who WMR previously reported was provided sanctuary in Qatar by the Qatari Interior Ministry, for whom Rudolph Giuliani's security company had a security contract, resulted in a stampede on a bridge over the Tigris River. The bridge collapsed from the panicked crowd and 840 people were killed. The incident caused Talabani to urge the elimination of mortars stockpiled in Iraq.

WMR sources also report that the US military also once secretly shipped 99 Glock silencers into Iraq, the purpose of which is not known but silencers are normally used for assassinations.

The story of the U.S. military's support for terrorism in Iraq took an even darker turn. A few months after the previous report, WMR had a disturbing follow-up, one that comports with later involvement by Petraeus, as CIA director, with Al Qaeda elements in Libya and Syria:

WMR has learned from an intelligence source who served in 2007 at the Tallil Air Base in Iraq, also known as Camp Adder by the U.S. Army and Ali Air Base by the U.S. Air Force, that United States intelligence services imported Afghan mercenaries into Iraq in order to attack Iraqi civilians and military personnel, as well as coalition forces, including U.S. service personnel. The Afghans were recruited from Taliban ranks and were paid for their services in Iraq.

WMR has learned that during 2007, Iraqi police stopped a truck hauling a 40-foot trailer on the Kerrada Bridge in Baghdad. When the Iraqi police officers checked the truck's trailer they were amazed to discover between 30 and 40 Afghan Taliban. They said they were brought into Iraq by the United States and were tasked with stirring up trouble in Iraq., much of it ascribed by U.S. military commanders as the work of the dubiously-named *Tanzim Qaidat al-Jihad fi Bilad al-Rafidayn* (Organization of Jihad's Base in the Country of the Two Rivers) or, more commonly known as "Al Qaeda of Mesopotamia."

The Iraqi police were told by senior U.S. military commanders on the scene to allow the Afghani insurgents to depart the Kerrada Bridge without any further hindrance.

The Taliban cell in Iraq apparently operated in conjunction with a covert U.S. plan to look the other way as Mahdi Army cells planted bombs in Iraq. On April 9, 2009, WMR reported: "WMR has been informed by a former private military contractor in Iraq that the United States was aware of the identities and even the cell phone numbers of several bomb making operatives within Muqtada al Sadr's Mahdi Army. The bomb cells were responsible for detonating a number of bombs in Iraq that targeted Sunnis and coalition personnel, including Americans." The failure of Generals David Petraeus and George Casey to act against the bomb-making cell was to not put in jeopardy a six-month extension of a cease-fire agreement agreed to by the MNF-I [Multi-national Force-Iraq] and [Muqtada] al Sadr's Shi'a militia in 2006.

One of the Shi'a bomb-making cells was located in the Kerrada district of Baghdad, the same area where the Taliban truck was stopped in Iraqi police. WMR has obtained a list provided to U.S. authorities by the coordinator of the Kerrada bomb cell. No action was taken by U.S. intelligence or military personnel to curtail the Shi'a militia bomb-making operation.

An English translation of the bomb-making cell list follows:

My name is Fadil Salim Naji of Jaderiya 923/43 Baghdad, Mobile 07901289687.

Before 2003 I was a Baathist party member and co-ordinator with the Iraqi government to the Iranian government. Since this time I have been working with the Iranian government in co-ordination with the Jeshil Mehdi army. My role has been to take money for arms purchases for the Mehdi army from the Iranian Intelligence and to place orders for weaponry. My meeting point with the Iranians was at the border point near to Maraghen City Iran....My orders were always from Athora City in Kerrada where I had contact to the Medhi army leaders.

> Akiel Salam Hamid nicknamed (Al Iranie) of Jaderiya Baghdad works with his father Hussein Salim Hamid who and are responsible for bomb making and arranging the planting of devices. Mobile 07702 668 185.,Land line govt issued – 7786495.
>
> Hussein Salim Hamid is responsible for counting military vehicles in the area of Jaderiya and is the main planning officer for appointing targets and building roadside bombs including the use of mainly semtex. He made the recent bomb which exploded outside the ice cream shop on Jaderiya street. Mobile – 0780 341 1480.
>
> Fathil Dabus, Basin Hyder/Salim No23 ? was told by Hussein Hamid he had three days to leave his job or he and his family would be killed. Fathil Mobile- 079067 61723 of Athora City received two calls from Hussein Hamid 23/10/07 and 11/10/07.
>
> Fathil Dabus wife also threatened by Hussein Hamid in front of the Azur Girls school Jaderiya.
>
> Mr Rand Badri a supervisor teacher was killed a week ago by Hussein Salim Hamid and also Rand's father the headmaster at the school was killed by Hussein Salim Hamid.
>
> Fadil – Mobile 078016 575 66 Another leader of the Mehdi army.
>
> Ziuna City – 079022 72814 – Mobile of an assassin working for Hussein Hamid.
>
> The reg on the car No.26888 BMW white test Baghdad. A car used to transport arms from the border meet point.
>
> Saed Ahmed 07902272814 Enforcer for Hussein Hamid and responsible for many killings and bombs in the area

The use by U.S. special operations forces and covert U.S. intelligence agents of Taliban fighters from Afghanistan and Mahdi Army insurgents to foment violence and terrorism in Iraq represents yet another serious violation of international and domestic anti-terrorism treaties and laws by the Bush-Cheney administration. In the case of using Taliban fighters to stage attacks on U.S., coalition, and Iraqi targets and blaming them on "Al Qaeda in Mesopotamia," the Bush-Cheney administration once again has demonstrated that "Al Qaeda" is as much an invention of the last administration as the billing of "9/11" as a foreign terrorist attack.

There were also credible reports linking Petraeus to the terrorist activities of the Mohajedin-e-Khaliq (MEK) in Iran. The MEK enjoyed the protection of Petraeus's forces in refugee camps in Iraq that were targeted by the pro-Iranian political leaders of Iraq. But Petraeus reportedly went even further in his support for the group, designated at the time as a Foreign Terrorist Organization by the U.S. State Department.

On May 19, 2008, WMR reported the following on the MEK:

> May 19, 2008 – Behind the anti-Iran terror network: the same people who brought us the Iraq war
>
> Iran has rolled up a western intelligence ring that not only planned a series of terrorist attacks in Iran but was responsible for a bombing on April 12 of a mosque center in Shiraz that killed 13 people and injured over 190 others. Iran foiled the intelligence ring's plans to bomb religious, scientific and educational institutions in Khuzestan, where there is a U.S- and British-supported secessionist movement; Fars; West Azerbaijan; Gilan, and the capital city of Tehran. Among the targets were the Tehran International Book Fair, the Russian Consulate in Gilan; oil pipelines; and other "soft targets."
>
> The plotters were caught with high explosives, cyanide, maps, and photos and sketches of targets.
>
> Although Iran is claiming the CIA was in charge of the group, the evidence and past practices strongly suggests that it was the neocon-supported Mojahedin-e-Khalq (MEK), or People's Mojahedin of Iran (PMOI), a State Department-designated terrorist group, that was behind the planned and past terrorist attacks. The MEK has received support and sanctuary from the United States in U.-occupied Iraq and the plan to launch terrorist attacks by the group bore more of the watermark of the new U.S. Central Command head General David Petraeus than the CIA. In fact, WMR has learned that any provocation against Iran is strongly opposed by key elements of the CIA's Directorate of Operations, particularly the Clandestine Services branch.
>
> US defense intelligence experts see the MEK as a cult-like organization similar to Pol Pot's Khmer Rouge in Cambodia. The MEK has, in the past,

received the support of the Soviet Union and Iraq's Saddam Hussein. It now enjoys the patronage of Iraq's Kurdish President Jalal Talabani.

However, it is the support the MEK receives from neocon pro-Israelis close to the Bush-Cheney regime that allows it to pursue bold operations like the planned terrorist attacks in Iran. In a paper written by US Marine Corps Major Adam Strickland for the Marine Corps Command and Staff College, it is pointed out that treatment of the MEK as a terrorist organization has not received support at home. The paper states: "In January 2004, former Assistant Secretary of Defense Richard Perle spoke at a fund raiser for victims of the Bam earthquake with Maryam Rajavi."

Rajavi is a co-founder of the MEK. Perle is a top policymaker for the neocon American Enterprise Institute (AEI) and according to a French intelligence officer who spoke to WMR, "Perle's telephone conversations from his villa in the south of France to his friends in Israel and Washington have been of great interest to us." The source said transcripts of the conversations were handed over by France to the FBI.

The MEKI has also been supported by the Washington Institute for Near East Policy (WINEP), another pro-Israel organization headed by Dennis Ross, now a top adviser to the Barack Obama campaign.

Iran has repeatedly offered to turn over Al Qaeda members it is holding in return for MEK terrorists in US custody. However, the Bush-Cheney regime has rejected all the offers.

The CIA treats any "intelligence" from the MEK and its allies, particularly those close to Israel, concerning Iran as bogus. Former Rep. Curt Weldon (R-PA), House Intelligence Committee ranking member Peter Hoekstra (R-MI), and former US ambassador to the UN John Bolton have all proffered "intelligence" on Iran's nuclear program from Fereidoun Mahdavi, also known as "Ali," who is an agent provocateur for Manucher Ghorbanifar, an Iran-Contra figure who is on the CIA's "burn list" as a fabricator, along with Iraq's "Curveball" and Ahmad Chalabi.

Ghorbanifar is close to the Pentagon's former neocon cell of Perle, Michael Ledeen (also of the American Enterprise Institute), Douglas Feith, and Harold Rhode. However, the CIA's former Paris station chief Bill Murray has warned that "intelligence" on Iran's nuclear program offered up about Iran by Mahdavi has been fabricated. The Committee for a Democratic Iran (CDI) is a clone of AIPAC and has been linked to both the MEK; the

MEK's political wing, the National Council of Resistance of Iran (NCRI), and Israel's Mossad intelligence agency.

The MEK also enjoys the support of members of the American Jewish community, particularly members of Congress. Major Strickland's paper contains the following December 2001 statement regarding the MEK by Rep. Gary Ackerman (D-NY), a strong supporter of the American Israel Public Affairs Committee (AIPAC) and Hillary Clinton:

"I don't give a shit if they are undemocratic. OK, so the MEK is a terrorist organization based in Iraq, which is a terrorist state. They are fighting Iran, which is another terrorist state. I say let's help them fight each other as much as they want. Once they are destroyed, I can celebrate twice over."

Other supporters of the MEK include Rep. Bob Filner (D-CA), another friend of AIPAC; former Senator Robert Torricelli (D-NJ); Rep. Tom Tancredo (R-CO); Rep. Ileana Ros-Lehtinen (R-FL), yet another AIPAC supporter; and former Attorney General John Ashcroft.

Major Strickland provided a dossier on the terror background of the group that receives the support of the U.S. neocons and the Bush-Cheney regime:

- November 1971: MEK failed in an attempt to kidnap US ambassador to Iran Douglas MacArthur II.

- 1973: MEK bombed Radio City Cinema, Shell Oil, and Pan American Airlines building in Tehran.

- June 2, 1973: MEK murdered US Lt. Col. Lewis I. Hawkins.

- August 1973: MEK bombed the Jordanian embassy in Tehran.

- May 21, 1975: MEK murdered US Colonel Paul Shafer and Lt. Col. Jack Turner.

- August 28, 1976: MEK murdered Rockwell International employees Donald G. Smith; Robert R. Krongard; and William C. Cottrell.

- November 4, 1975: MEK participated in US embassy seizure in Tehran.

- September 3, 1981: MEK bombed Islamic Republic Party headquarters killing President Mohammed Ali Rajai, Prime Minister Hojatolislam Mohammad Javad Bahonar, and Chief Justice Ayatollah Mohammed Beheshti, along with 14 ministers and 27 Majlis deputies.

- September 1, 1998: Iran announced it had substantial proof that the Taliban was providing logistical support to the MEK [this was at the same time Osama bin Laden was operating under Taliban protection in Afghanistan].

- April 11, 1999; MEK murdered Lt. Gen. Ali Sayyad-Shirazi, the Iranian Deputy Chief of Staff and Iran's most decorated soldier.

- February 2000: MEK mortared offices used by Supreme Leader Grand Ayatollah Khamanei and former President Hashemi Rafsanjani during "Operation Grand Bahman."

- May 2000: MEK murdered Rear Adm. Abdollah Roudaki, a senior commander of the Iranian Revolutionary Guard Corps.

The MEK also funded some of its activities through it being a beneficiary of Saddam Hussein's UN Oil-for-Food program. The charges were contained in Charles Duelfer's report on Iraq's weapons of mass destruction. MEK camps at Camp Fallujah in Saddam's Iraq were also reportedly used to house Iraqi weapons.

The MEK, supported by the neocons, has been caught by Iran in a major terrorist plot. The CIA's fingerprints are not on this plot, although CIA Director Michael Hayden, an ally of the neocons and Dick Cheney, may be aware of it and may have even provided "off-the-books" support. Iran must look at the true plotters at the AEI, AIPAC, and Mossad's headquarters in Herzliya, Israel.

Under Petraeus's watch, U.S. small arms began flooding into Iraq. This story was covered by WMR in June 2009:

<u>June 22, 2009 – Pentagon purposely flooded Iraq and Afghanistan with trackable small arms</u>

WMR has learned from informed sources that during the Bush administration, the Department of Defense purposely flooded small arms into war zones in Iraq and Afghanistan in order to track their whereabouts and identify insurgent groups that came into possession of the weapons. It is not known whether the covert weapons proliferation program is continuing under the Obama administration.

The Pentagon's highly-classified program used contractors as middlemen to broker the sale of smuggled weapons into the Iraq and Afghanistan war zones, WMR has been told. Smuggled weapons were fitted with radio frequency identification (RFID) devices to enable tracking by U.S. electronic intelligence (ELINT) systems operated by the National Security Agency (NSA). RFIDs use chips that emit a unique electronic signal when scanned. The covert weapons tracking program reportedly involves the large NSA contractor, Booz Allen Hamilton.

RFID tracking technology is already being used by the Department of Energy to track nuclear materials during storage and transport.

An apparent tip-off on the program is contained in an October 23, 2008, letter from President George Bush to relevant congressional committee senior members:

TEXT OF A LETTER FROM THE PRESIDENT

TO THE CHAIRMEN AND RANKING MEMBERS OF

THE HOUSE AND SENATE COMMITTEES ON ARMED SERVICES,

THE CHAIRMAN AND RANKING MEMBERS OF

THE HOUSE COMMITTEE ON FOREIGN AFFAIRS,

THE SENATE COMMITTEE ON FOREIGN RELATIONS, AND

THE SENATE COMMITTEE ON BANKING, HOUSING, AND URBAN AFFAIRS

October 23, 2008

Dear Mr. Chairman: (Dear Representative) (Dear Senator)

Pursuant to section 1228(b) of the National Defense Authorization Act for Fiscal Year 2008, Public Law 110-181 (NDAA), I hereby certify that a registration and monitoring system for defense articles provided to the Government of Iraq or any other group, organization, citizen, or resident

> of Iraq, meeting the requirements set forth in subsection 1228(c) of the NDAA, has been established.
>
> Specifically, I certify that the registration and monitoring system herein referenced includes:
>
> 1. the registration of the serial numbers of all small arms to be provided to the Government of Iraq or to other groups, organizations, citizens, or residents of Iraq;
>
> 2. a program of end-use monitoring of all lethal defense articles provided to such entities or individuals; and
>
> 3. the maintenance of a detailed record of the origin, shipping, and distribution of all defense articles transferred under the Iraq Security Forces Fund or any other security assistance program to such entities or individuals.
>
> Sincerely,
>
> GEORGE W. BUSH

Defense Department contractors also have apparently attempted to entrap U.S. civilian and military personnel into selling smuggled weapons to U.S. private security contractors acting as legitimate brokers in Iraq, Afghanistan, and Pakistan. In one case, a contractor for the Drug Enforcement Administration (DEA) was asked by a U.S. private security contractor to sell him Austrian-made 9 mm Glocks equipped with silencers. Smelling a setup, the DEA contractor refused to cooperate.

One of the firms involved in the clandestine weapons business is allegedly Taos Industries of Huntsville, Alabama. The firm specializes in obtaining foreign military systems for the Defense Intelligence Agency (DIA). According to a 2008 Amnesty International report, Taos is the biggest private small arms supplier to Iraq since the U.S. invasion and occupation in 2003. In 2006, Taos, a Delaware corporation, was bought by Agility, a Kuwait-based and owned firm. Taos is headed up by retired Army Lt. Gen. Joseph Cosumano, who, after retiring from the Army in 2004 served as an executive of Kellogg, Brown & Root (KBR), the firm once headed by Dick Cheney.

Taos was started by David Hogan after he retired in 1989 as the chief of foreign intelligence for the U.S. Army Missile Command at the Redstone

Arsenal in Huntsville, Alabama. Hogan eventually turned over the company to his two sons, Craig and Steven. In January 2005, Craig Hogan, the President of Taos and his brother Steven, the chief financial officer of the firm, died in the crash of their single-engine plane shortly after takeoff from Huntsville International Airport. David Hogan stepped down as chairman and CEO after selling the firm to PWC Logistics of Alexandria, Virginia in 2006. PWC, along with other companies in the Kuwait-owned PWC Group, including GeoLogistics, TransOceanic, and Trans-Link, changed their names to Agility in November 2006.

According to the Small Arms Survey in 2007 other Pentagon contractors that supplied non-NATO weapons, such as Kalashnikovs, to Iraqi forces included Keisler Police Supply of Jeffersonville, Indiana; Golden Wings; ANHAM Joint Venture of Vienna, Virginia (for which A. Huda Farouki, a friend and former business partner of Iraqi con artist Ahmad Chalabi was a principal); AEY of Miami; Defense Logistics Service; Blane International Group of Cumming, Georgia, which had experience in obtaining weapons systems from Ukraine; and International Trading Establishment of Amman, Jordan, a consortium of Czech, Spanish and Jordanian corporations, which subcontracted to Poly-Technologies of Beijing. Poly-Technologies, which did business in the United States as Dynasty Holding of Atlanta and whose representative in the United States was retired Chinese People's Liberation Army General Bao Ping "Robert" Ma, was charged twice in the 1990s with smuggling AK-47s and accessories into the United States.

On June 20, 2008, AEY, Inc. corporate officials Efraim Diveroli, David Packouz, Alexander Podrizki, and Ralph Merrill were indicted by a federal grand jury in Miami for supplying the U.S. Army with faulty ammunition for Afghan security forces. The indictment stated that AEY officials "submitted documents to the Army falsely attesting that the ammunition they were providing was manufactured and originated in Albania, when, in fact, the ammunition came from China. To effectuate the scheme, defendants Efraim Diveroli, David Packouz, and Alexander Podrizki would direct others to assist in the packaging of ammunition to be delivered to Afghanistan, and would provide instructions to remove Chinese markings from containers in order to conceal that the ammunition was manufactured and originated in China . . . With each shipment, Diveroli, on behalf of AEY would falsely certify in a Certificate of Conformance that the ammunition being furnished conformed with the contract requirements, and that the manufacturer and point of origin of the ammunition was the Military Export and Import Company (hereinafter referred to as MEICO) in Tirana, Albania."

In 2005 it was revealed that thousands of Italian Beretta pistols shipped from Italy via a British firm, Super Vision International, to a U.S. base in Iraq the previous year, were found at an "Al Qaeda" arms cache in Iraq. The weapons were originally supplied to U.S. forces in Iraq by Taos under a Defense Department contract. Some 20,000 of the pistols were discovered in the hands of loyalists to Abu Musab al-Zarqawi, the late head of the "Al Qaeda" faction in Iraq.

A 2007 Government Accountability Office (GAO) report stated that some 190,000 U.S.-supplied small arms were "unaccounted for" in Iraq. Most of the weapons were AK-47s procured from Bulgaria with the assistance of the U.S. Defense Attache in Sofia. The DIA reportedly approved the weapons deal facilitated through the state-owned Bulgarian arms firm Kintex.

In April 2004, the opposition Indian Congress Party charged that Bharatiya Janata Party (BJP) Home Affairs Minister L. K. Advani with smuggling AK-47s from Bulgaria. The Statesman of India newspaper reported on April 9, 2004, "The Congress released fresh set of documents to reinforce its allegation that the home ministry had rejected the offer of the lowest bidder and awarded the contract to a 'dubious' Bulgarian company Kintex. Mr Sibal alleged that 'Kintex has links with the globally-notorious illicit arms supplier, Tajikistan-born V.A. Bout, as well as the suppliers of the arms dropped at Purulia.' He declined to disclose the deal's beneficiaries though he had earlier alleged that 'the son of a top BJP leader had received kickbacks just like someone who is almost like a son to another top BJP leader was engaged in such deals earlier.'"

The 2008 Amnesty International report also stated that Taos used sub-contractors cited by the United Nations for weapons smuggling. One of the companies used by Taos was Aerocom, a Moldovan/Ukrainian company. Aerocom shipped 99 tons of weapons, mostly AK-47 rifles, from Bosnia to Iraqi security forces in 2005 under a contract to Taos. Scout, a Croatian brokerage firm used by Aerocom in shipping weapons, was not even registered in Croatia.

Aerocom was linked to the global weapons smuggling empire of "Lord of War" Viktor Bout, now in prison in Thailand and subject to legal proceedings that may see him extradited to the United States to face charges that he attempted to sell weapons to Colombian FARC guerrillas. Bout contends that he was the victim of a setup.

On December 11, 2005, WMR reported: "One Chisinau, Moldova-based Bout front company, Aerocom, which also does business as Air Mero, is contracted to fly for Kellogg, Brown & Root in Iraq and elsewhere. Aerocom has also been cited in UN and DEA reports for being involved in drug smuggling in Belize. Some law enforcement officials in the United States and Europe believe that the covert flights being operated by CIA contractors and Bout's companies in support of secret prisoner movement are also involved in smuggling drugs. After being subjected to news reports, Aerocom quickly changed its name last year."

The attempt by U.S. private security contractors to "sting" DEA agents abroad in weapons smuggling deals may be linked to the DEA agents getting too close to the convergence of covert weapons and drug smuggling by the U.S. government.

Considering Bout's knowledge of the covert and classified U.S. program to sell traceable weapons around the world, his fears that the United States wants to put him in a "Super Max" prison and away from potential book publishers may be well-founded.

Another shadowy firm used by the U.S. to transport weapons to Iraq and Somalia for insurgent use was Serbia-based Air Tomisko, which reportedly regularly flew weapons from Serbia for the U.S. to Baghdad and Basra.

Some of the weapons supplied to Iraq by the Pentagon have also ended up in the hands of insurgent groups in neighboring countries, including the Kurdish Workers Party (PKK) in Turkey and the Mojahehdin-e-Khalq (MEK) in Iran. The person who was in charge of the Iraqi security training program during most of the small weapons "loss" was General David Petraeus, now the chief of the U.S. Central Command (CENTCOM).

The clandestine program to place electronically-traceable weapons into the hands of insurgent groups is continuing, according to our sources. The latest hot area is Somalia where Glocks and shot guns being smuggled to Somali "pirates." The Somali waters piracy has been a boon for private security companies with maritime cargo and cruise line companies anxious to contract out security for their vessels to the plethora of firms offering armed protection services.

WMR has also received information that Blackwater, now Xe, was also involved in the clandestine weapons program. In 2007, Blackwater was subject to a federal investigation for weapons smuggling in Iraq after two of the firm's former employees pleaded guilty to possession of stolen firearms involved in foreign commerce. After the two ex-employees, Kenneth Wayne Cashwell of Virginia Beach, Virginia and William Ellsworth "Max" Grumiaux of Clemmons, North Carolina, agreed to cooperate with prosecutors, the Departments of Justice, State, and Commerce began fully investigating the company for unauthorized arms shipments to "police training" facilities in Jordan and Iraq.

Bout was eventually captured by U.S. authorities in Thailand and he was convicted on a variety of federal charges and sentenced to 25 years in prison (the minimum sentence that could have been given).

Be it the Mahdi Army in Iraq, Taliban units exported from Afghanistan to Iraq, Salafists and Al Qaeda in Libya, weapons smuggling to irregular combatants, or the MEK in Iraq and Iran, Petraeus was more than willing to cut deals with groups that had the blood of thousands of Americans and tens of thousands of other nationals on their hands. The reader might appreciate how the author cringed every time a senator or congressman uttered the words, "the great General Petraeus."

Petraeus also presided over one of the largest military outsourcing frenzies ever seen by the military. Erik Prince's Blackwater, alone, accounted for billions of dollars in contracts in Iraq and Afghanistan under Petraeus's watch.

Blackwater Group operated under various brass plates and corporate identities around the world:

The Prince Group (holding company)
Blackwater USA → Xe Services LLC
Blackwater Worldwide → Xe Services
Prince Manufacturing
Total Intelligence Solutions (TIS), LLC
The Black Group (merged to form TIS)
The Terrorism Research Center, Inc. (merged to form TIS)
Technical Defense (merged to form TIS)
Blackwater Lodge & Training Center → US Training Center
Blackwater Airships, LLC → Guardian Flight Systems
Blackwater Maritime Solutions
Raven Development Group
Blackwater Target Systems → GSD Manufacturing
Blackwater Security Consulting
Blackwater Peace and Stability Operations Institute
Blackwater K-9
Aviation Worldwide Services (AWS) → AAR Corporation

```
STI Aviation, Inc. (subsidiary of AWS)
Air Quest, Inc.                  "
Presidential Airways, Inc.
Blackwater SELECT (Karachi)
 Kestral Holdings (Pakistani partner)
   Kestral Logistics
   Kestral Trading
Blackwater PTC
Paravant, LLC.
XPG
E&J Holdings LLC
Greystone, Ltd. (Barbados)
 Satelles Solutions, Inc. (Philippines)
Constellation Consulting
Grupo Tactico (Chile) (partner) → Red Tactica Consulting Group, Washington, DC
 Neskowin (Uruguay) (recruiter)
 Global Guards (Panama) (recruiter) → Gun Supply (Lima) → Triple Canopy → Your
Solutions, Inc. (Honduran recruiter) → Clayton Consultants → AIG
TigerSwan (spin-off)
 Babylon Eagles/TigerSwan (Iraqi joint venture)
Sovereign Military Order of Malta (diplomatic cover)
```

With Petraeus's previous connections to Blackwater, renamed Xe Services and then Academi, various insurgent groups and Al Qaeda elements throughout the Middle East, and the government of Qatar, and his more recent control over the CIA and Pentagon special operations elements, calling on the assistance of such friends and allies to arrange for a "crisis" in Benghazi would have been a cinch.

It is noteworthy that the reported involvement of Qatari government officials with terrorists in Iraq would be repeated in 2011 with Qatar's support for terrorists in Libya, followed by similar support for Islamist terrorists in Syria in 2012. Yet Qatar also serves as a major CENTCOM base, where Petraeus resided for long periods of time when he was in command.

Just as in Pakistan, there were reports that Israel backed some of the most extreme elements among the Libyan opposition, especially in Cyrenaica, with its capital of Benghazi, where Israel reportedly had long-range designs to re-establish a economically-dominant Jewish community.

In any event, no CIA conspiracy is complete without the presence of shadowy figures that transcend CIA dirty operations through the decades. Romney put together an impressive list of retired flag rank military officers who acted under the title of the "Romney For President Military Advisory Council."[See page 107] Or was the council, considering the plot against Obama from his active duty flag and field grade officers, more like the fictitious Emergency COMmunications CONtrol – ECOMCON – from the military coup novel "Seven Days in May?" One name on the Romney lost stands out like a sore thumb, that of retired Air Force Major General Richard Secord, of not only Iran-contra infamy but of the template of the plot against Obama, the October Surprise plot against Jimmy Carter.

Chapter 7 – Petraeus: A general with little respect from his troops

General Petraeus may have enthralled and enraptured those from Paula Broadwell to Senators McCain, Graham, and Lieberman, but he did not command the same kind of admiration from his troops in the field. WMR had long tracked Petraeus based on sources within the military who served under Petraeus. The following reports are from their stories from the battlefields:

> March 17, 2008 – Winter Soldier reveals subservience of US troops to contractors in Iraq and malfeasance of John McCain's "great General Petraeus."
>
> U.S. Army veterans of Iraq revealed how they were subservient to U.S. contractors in Iraq and were ordered to put their own lives on the line to improve the bottom line of Halliburton, the one-time parent company of Defense Department contractor Kellogg, Brown & Root (KBR).
>
> The veterans of Iraq testified at Winter Soldier 2008 held in Silver Spring in suburban Washington from March 14 through 16.
>
> Kelly Dougherty, a veteran of a Colorado National Guard military police unit in Iraq said that upon her unit's entry into Iraq in late March 2003, their duties primarily consisted of military convoy escort and patrols. Soon, they were assigned convoy escort and protection duties for KBR convoys from Kuwait.
>
> By the summer of 2003, Dougherty's unit was stationed at Tallil airbase, south of Nasariyah. More and more problems were experienced with KBR convoy trucks. The trucks frequently broke down and Dougherty's unit was ordered to secure the trucks and their cargo from desperate Iraqi civilians who wanted to loot the trucks, especially of much needed diesel fuel and food. The Army was told that the trucks and their contents were "U.S. assets" and Dougherty's unit was to protect them with "deadly force." Halliburton and KBR are the firms for which Vice President Dick

Cheney once served as President and CEO and Cheney continued to have a vested financial interest in the companies at the time of the invasion and occupation of Iraq.

KBR trucks were re-routed from a major highway from Kuwait to Baghdad called "MSR (Main Supply Route) Jackson" to MSR Tampa, a smaller highway. Dougherty's unit was ordered to guard more KBR trucks that broke down, became stuck in the mud, or were involved in accidents.

Dougherty's unit received conflicting orders. They were alternately ordered to protect the vehicles and to leave the vehicles. Iraqi civilians wanted to liberate the disabled vehicles of their fuel, tires, or doors to use or to sell. Because of cost and rationing, Iraqi civilians were in desperate need of diesel fuel on the trucks. Dougherty said her unit operated under the conflicting orders into 2004.

Dougherty said she and her unit often used rubber bullets, bean bag pellet ammunition, and concussion grenades against Iraqi men and boys who were trying to get much needed fuel and food from disabled KBR trucks. However, the standing orders were to burn off all the fuel and destroy the trucks. Dougherty said U.S. Army MPs were ordered to risk their lives and the lives of innocent Iraqis to guarantee a profit for KBR.

In one case, Dougherty said her unit destroyed an ambulance that fell off a truck in an area where there were no ambulances and where the local village elders volunteered to repair the ambulance and restore it to use. In another case, she and her unit burned a truck and its cargo of produce in front of hungry Iraqis desperate for food.

Dougherty also testified that Third Country Nationals (TCNs) hired by companies like KBR to drive trucks in convoys were treated horribly by the firm. She said drivers from countries such as the Philippines, India, and Tibet had their passports held by KBR to guarantee they did not leave their jobs.

When Dougherty's unit departed Iraq in February 2004 they were billeted in Camp Arifjan in Kuwait, a tent city run by KBR. Dougherty said their yellow tents were covered with a thick black and reeking mold that resulted in respiratory infections. Dougherty said her unit was forced to live in the moldy tents for two weeks prior to transport back to the United States.

Former Army Captain Luis Carlos Montalvan also discovered contract malfeasance that is directly attributable to General David Petraeus, the current US commander in Iraq. Montalvan's unit was ordered to guard the Syria-Iraq Al Waleed point of entry (POE) no man's land of 100 kilometers and a wide swath of the Al Anbar desert with 30 to 40 troops. Montalvan said his complaints of inadequate resources fell on deaf ears. He added that General Ricardo Sanchez and Coalition Provisional Authority head Paul "Jerry" Bremer were incompetent when it came to what was going on outside of Baghdad.

After leaving the service, Montalvan was asked, in January 2007, to be the Iraq Security expert for the Iraq Planning Group at the American Enterprise Institute (AEI), the neocon think tank that came up with the idea for the Iraq "surge." Montalvan came to the attention of AEI because while he was on active duty he wrote a January 14, 2007, OP ED in the *New York Times* titled "Losing Iraq, One Truckload at a Time."

Montalvan said because he was still on active duty, his article dealt with Iraqi corruption. However, what he could not write about then but testified about at Winter Soldier was that the "crumb trail of Iraqi corruption led to American corruption." He added that the corruption involves current and retired American colonels and generals.

Montalvan described corruption with a contract over which three top generals in Iraq, all supporters of the neocon policy of AEI's [American Enterprise Institute] and the Bush administration's surge, are implicated. Montalvan said there was no guidance from the US-run Civilian Police Assistance Training (CPAT) program on issuing police equipment to the Iraqi police. The Iraqi police training program involved three U.S. Army generals – Joseph Fil, the Commanding General of the CPAT team; Kevin Bergner, the deputy commander of coalition forces in northwestern Iraq in 2005; and David Petraeus, the Commander of the Multi-National Security

Transition Command Iraq (MSTCI). Presumptive Republican presidential candidate John McCain has frequently lauded the "great General Petraeus."

Montalvan said that one warehouse run by Lee Dynamics International (LDI) was to procure, store, and distribute equipment for the Iraqi police. However, the contract, for which LDI received billions of dollars, was non-existent because it was Iraqi police officials, not LDI personnel, who were in charge of the "LDI warehouse." Petraeus, who was in charge of CPAT and MSTCI, did not ensure any accountability for LDI and other contractors. LDI, formerly known as American Logistics Services, was suspended by the US Army after it was caught paying bribes to US Army officers in Kuwait. In December 2006, Major Gloria Davis, a U.S. Army contracting officer in Kuwait, allegedly shot herself in a suicide after being accused of accepting $225,000 in bribes from LDI. The firm was also accused of paying bribes to Army officers in Iraq who were in charge of training the Iraqi police. The officers identified in the investigation of LDI worked closely with Petraeus.

If one were to mention the name Ted Westhusing around Petraeus, they would certainly get a reaction. Westhusing was the Army's top expert on ethics. He did not come back from Iraq alive. The following is the tragic story about Westhusing, as reported by WMR:

January 23, 2006 – More details emerge on Col. Ted Westhusing's "suiciding" in Iraq.

Days before his supposed suicide by a "self-inflicted" gunshot wound in a Camp Dublin, Iraq trailer, West Point Honor Board member and Iraqi police and security forces trainer Col. Ted Westhusing reported in e-mail to the United States that "terrible things were going on in Iraq." He also said he hoped he would make it back to the United States alive. Westhusing had three weeks left in his tour of duty in Iraq when he allegedly shot himself in June 2005.

It is noteworthy that after Westhusing's death, two top Army generals, both responsible for training Iraqi forces, General Dave Petraeus, the Commander of the Multi National Security Transition Command Iraq (MNSTCI), and Maj. Gen. Joseph Fil, the Commander of the 1st Cavalry

Division, were quickly transferred without much fanfare to Fort Leavenworth, Kansas and Fort Hood, Texas, respectively.

Informed sources report that Westhusing was prepared to blow the whistle on fraud involving US Investigations Services (USIS), a Carlyle Group company, when he died. He had also discovered links between USIS principals and clandestine events involving the Iran-Contra scandal of the Reagan-Bush I administrations. Westhusing has also linked USIS to the illegal killing and torture of Iraqis. USIS personnel whom Westhusing was investigating had the keys to his trailer. In addition, Westhusing's personal bodyguard was given a leave of absence shortly before the colonel's death.

The U.S. Army's official report on Westhusing's death contained a number of falsehoods, according to those close to the case. Most importantly, the Army report stated that Westhusing had electronically communicated an interest in obtaining hollow point bullets. The bullet which killed Westhusing was a hollow point. However, the Army's statement was false, according to an informed source. In addition, the Army combed Westhusing's service record and interviewed a number of colleagues in order to concoct a story that would make suicide appear plausible.

California Democratic Senator Barbara Boxer is reportedly trying to get the Senate to investigate Westhusing's death. However, with the Republicans in firm control, it appears that murder of senior U.S. military officers is also something the GOP is more than willing to cover up.

The reality of Petraeus's decisions were obviously lost on many journalists who found it more beneficial to their job security to laud the general and ignore the horrors of Petraeus's much-heralded "surges" and "counter-insurgency" strategies.

Petraeus was also a fan of Iraqi opposition fabulist and fraudster Ahmed Chalabi, the neocon darling and head of the Iraqi National Congress who produced the source for phony intelligence on Iraq's alleged WMDs, the hoaxer known as "Curveball." Petraeus's high opinion of Chalabi during the "surge" in Iraq, was expressed by Boylan, Petraeus's mouthpiece, "[Chalabi] is an important part of the process." [46]

---

[46] Nancy A. Youssef, "Chalabi back in action in Iraq," McClatchy Newspapers, October 28, 2007.

L'Affaire Petraeus

After America's attention was riveted on the death and maiming that followed a crazed gunman's attack on the campus of Virginia Tech in April 2007, WMR put the tragedy into the perspective of the on-going tragedy of Iraq:

> April 17, 2007 – The reality of Iraq. The specter of sudden violent death or disabling permanent injury – such as that visited upon Virginia Tech by a crazed gunman yesterday – confronts our servicemen and women every day and every hour in war-torn Iraq.

WMR has learned the following facts of life from U.S. military members in Iraq, many of whom have just found out that their tours have been extended until December of this year. Many of our service members know that CNN, Fox, and the other corporate media are not reporting the truth from Iraq but are walking a fuzzy line between mouthing Bush administration propaganda and actual news reporting.

Iraq is locked in a bloody civil war in which Shias and Sunnis are prepared to massacre one another to the last person. The only thing they agree on is their hatred of the U.S. occupiers. The much-heralded Gen. David Petraeus is faced with an impossible situation in which alliances change on a daily basis. Take Tal Afar, for example.

While Kurds are trying to ethnically cleanse the primarily-Turkmen city and replace Turkmen with Kurds, the U.S. occupiers are trying to separate Shia and Sunni Turkmen into separate cantonments. However, the Turkmen, who are not Arab, are not plagued by the Shia-Sunni split that pits Iraqi Sunni and Shia Arabs against one another. Petraeus and his advisers are ignorant of this and many other facts of life in Iraq. The American military does not know enemy from friend. Female U.S. military police are just as likely as their male counterparts to be killed while on patrol. There are the rapes of female U.S. military members by their Iraqi police and military "allies," and fellow American troops. Add to this, substance abuse and murder among and between U.S. forces and their Iraqi "allies."

Most of the Iraqi police are corrupt and untrustworthy. Most U.S. troops who work with the Iraqi police do so armed and post guards in the event Iraqi police try to kill American troops. This unhappy marriage of convenience drawn up by neo-cons in Washington will continue for at least the next 15 months. The same situation exists between the U.S. military and the Iraqi Army, which is predominantly Shia militiamen, many loyal to Moqtada al Sadr, who has just pulled his ministers from the Nouri al Maliki government. When U.S. troops capture Sunni militiamen, they purposely do not release them to the Iraqi Army, lest they be massacred.

Most of Shia insurgents who are arrested are released back into their communities. There is not enough detention space for either Shias or Sunnis. And, as with the case of captured Sunnis, they are released rather than face execution by the Sunnis.

Nothing stops explosive formed penetrators (EFPs) used by the insurgents. They easily rip through up-armored Humvees like driving a Ginzu knife through a Coke can. What remains of U.S. soldiers hit with EFPs are hardly recognizable as human.

An additional 500,000 US troops in Iraq is the only surge that could even start to make a difference. Less only provides more cannon fodder for the enemy or "enemies." Over 170,000 US troops have served more than one tour in Iraq. Now, everyone in Iraq now must serve 15 months.

The Rules Of Engagement (ROE) for the U.S. military are now so strict that most units that are attacked never fire a shot in retaliation, even when they suffer fatalities among their own ranks.

Route clearance is now performed by 20-year old combat engineers. These engineers look for the EFP's and the Improvised Explosive Devices (IEDs) on roads used by military convoys. Roadside bombs are so well hidden they go off without being detected first. One such bomb recently misfired and killed around two dozen small school girls walking home, hand in hand, from school. The American combat engineers were not able to detect the bomb in time to save the girls. The American troops, especially the fathers, came to tears over the murder of the young girls. And the American troops could not even stop to give the girls first aid because they were on a rescue mission to assist a stranded American squad under fire.

Private sector contractors – the war profiteers from Blackwater, Halliburton, Triple Canopy, and all the others start, with less than three years of experience, at a salary of $86,000 for moving boxes around in a warehouse. Their active duty counterparts, with much more experience, earn $32,000 a year. However, the contractors can leave Iraq whenever they see fit.

Mental healthcare for U.S. troops leaving Iraq should be a top priority but it is not. They are left for an inadequate Defense and Veterans Affairs Departments to deal with.

Apparently, Petraeus was not even highly thought of when he was a Lieutenant Colonel. WMR ran the following story about Petraeus after he was chosen to head up CENTCOM:

November 3, 2008 – New CENTCOM commander shot in 1991 fragging incident

An informed U.S. Army source revealed to WMR that the former commander of U.S. forces in Iraq and the recently-installed chief of the U.S. Central Command (CENTCOM), General David Petraeus – who John McCain calls "our dear General Petraeus" – was the target of an enlisted man in a "fragging" incident during a live-fire training exercise at Fort Campbell, Kentucky in 1991.

Petraeus was hit in the chest and suffered lung damage when the enlisted man opened fire with his M-16 rifle. The Army officially referred to the incident as a "training accident." However, our Army source claims that was a cover-up.

Ironically, Petraeus, who nearly died from the shooting, was operated on at the Vanderbilt Medical Center in Nashville, Tennessee. Petraeus' surgeon turned out to be Dr. Bill Frist, who later was elected to the U.S. Senate and served as Senate Majority Leader.

The Frist connection is not Petraeus' only link to the Republican Party. Petraeus' close colleague is Army Colonel Michael Meese, the son of Ronald Reagan Attorney General Edwin Meese. Edwin Meese is now a major player in the Arlington, Virginia-based right-wing Christian cult called "The Fellowship." Tennessee Republican Senator Lamar Alexander has likened Petraeus to a modern-day General George Marshall. However, most of Petraeus' troops refer to him as General "Betray Us," and claim that he is nothing more than a bootlicker and ass kisser. In fact, Petraeus' predecessor as CENTCOM chief, Admiral William Fallon, reportedly told Petraeus that he thought he was "an ass-kissing little chickenshit."

Chickenshit as Petraeus may have been, the "ass-kissing," as Fallon put it, paid off. Petraeus was one of the attendees at the 2009 Bilderberg Conference held at theAstir Palace Hotel in the suburban Athens resort of Vouliagmeni. Bilderberg is where the movers and shakers of the world gather annually in different venues to scheme and plot off-the-record. Petraeus was able to run shoulders with old neocon pals like Project for the New American century co-founder Robert Kagan (married to Secretary of State Hillary Clinton's spokeswoman Victoria Nuland), special envoy to Afghanistan and Pakistan Richard Holbrooke, Richard Perle, Dennis Ross, and Paul Wolfowitz, but real power wielders like David Rockefeller, Henry Kissinger, BP Chairman Peter Sutherland, and fellow Army General Keith Alexander, director of the National Security Agency.

Whether the Bilderberg Group or the Council on Foreign relations, Petraeus understood where his allies were. One of his most loyal promoters was Max Boot, the neocon policy guru and CFR member. Boot came to Petraeus's defense after many believed Petraeus committed the arch-son for any politician or officer in Washington, uttering an anti-Israel statement. In Petraeus's case it was his testimony before the Senate Armed Services Committee. The transcript of Petraeus's remarks reads:

> "The enduring hostilities between Israel and some of its neighbors present distinct challenges to our ability to advance our interests... Israeli-Palestinian tensions often flare into violence and large-scale armed confrontations. The conflict foments anti-American sentiment, due to a perception of U.S. favoritism for Israel. Arab anger over the Palestinian question limits the strength and depth of U.S. partnerships with governments and peoples in the [region] and weakens the legitimacy of moderate regimes in the Arab world. Meanwhile, al-Qaeda and other militant groups exploit that anger to mobilize support."[47]

Some members of the "Support Israel At Any Cost" brigade immediately pounced on Petraeus for suggesting that America's tilt toward Israel was a liability for the United States. After Petraeus exchanged some e-mails with his friend Boot and Boot defended Petraeus in an article in the Jewish magazine *Commentary*, the fire was largely extinguished. [48]

After Petraeus's fall at the CIA, Boot wrote, "The graveyards are full of indispensable men," it's often said, meaning that few are genuinely indispensable. David H. Petraeus was one of the few, which is why his loss for the U.S. government, after his admission of adultery, is so tragic . . . Petraeus also urged young officers to get outside their intellectual comfort zone by going to civilian graduate schools and reading widely. Quite a few of his proteges followed his advice — including, it must be said, Paula Broadwell — but few of them could hope to match his success, in no small part because the Army, sadly, still regards excessive intellectualism as a debilitating defect. Perhaps Petraeus could have remade the military if he had been appointed chairman of the Joint

---

[47] Max Boot, "A Lie: David Petraeus, Anti-Israel," *Commentary*, March 18, 2010.
[48] Ibid.

Chiefs of Staff — a post he had earned — but President Obama preferred to shunt him off to the CIA where he would play a less public role. Now he is gone from the CIA too, and it is doubtful that the military will see his like for a long time to come."[49]

Some observers, propagandists, and conspiracy originators decided that Petraeus was set up by the "Israel Lobby" because of the testimony from 2010. However, Petraeus was defended by the very Lobby that was said to have deep-sixed him at the CIA. Boot's undying devotion to Petraeus is but one example of the high esteem neocons and Israeli supporters hold Petraeus.

---

[49] Max Boot, "Petraeus: A Necessary Man, " *Los Angeles Times*, November 13, 2012.

Afterword

This book represents a preliminary assessment on the Petraeus affair and its wider ramifications. Of course, it is too early to predict how the scandal will ultimately turn out.

But one thing is certain. As time elapses, so will the details of the attempt to oust Obama from the White House by a group of treasonous Republicans and mutinous military officers. In fact, by the first week of December, the Petraeus scandal was already losing steam in the corporate media with evening broadcast newscasts leading off with the fact that the Duchess of Cambridge, Kate Middleton, was pregnant with the future monarch of England.

It is amazing that after so much has been researched and written about plots against the American presidency over the years – from the conspiracy to assassinate Abraham Lincoln, to the plot to overthrow FDR, the conspiracy to assassinate President John F. Kennedy, the CIA's role in Watergate to dump Richard Nixon, and the October Surprise plot against Jimmy Carter, people find it difficult or impossible to believe that such a conspiracy existed to deny Obama a second term and usher into office a Romney administration.

In 1975, in the wake of Watergate, renegade CIA agent Phil Agee, who went into exile abroad after disclosing some of the CIA's dirtiest of secrets, wrote a fictional account of how the CIA might decide the outcome of the 1976 presidential election and insert into the Oval Office one of its own puppets.

Agee wrote about a fictional but very realistic meeting at Langley between the DCI (Director of Central Intelligence), IG (Inspector General), DDO (Deputy Director of Operations), DDM&S (Deputy Director of Management and Services. The plot to elect a president of the CIA's choosing was to be code-named PBPRIME, the actual CIA cryptonym for the United States of America.

The following is an abridged version of Agee's article. It should be pointed out that in 1975, the leading Democratic presidential candidates were Alabama Governor George Wallace, reformed after his near assassination in 1972 as a moderate Democrat who supported civil rights and affirmative action, and

Senator Henry "Scoop" Jackson, the war hawk from Washington state. Agee refers to Jackson in the article as "Henry Scooperman":

April 1975

DCI: If we're going to do anything about the possibilities I outlined last week, we've got to get started. You've all had five days to think it over and if any of you want to opt out now, I'll understand. We can talk freely here. Stan?

IG: I'm for it. We've got to do something and I think your analysis is dead on. Having the agency get into the 1976 elections makes all kinds of sense. Congress and the press are really turning up the heat and the agency has got to counterattack somehow.

DDO: You know, I always thought Truman had that phrase wrong. Our motto should be: "If you can't stand the heat, snuff the flames." [Laughter]

DCI: What are your thoughts, Bob?

DDM&S: Yeah, I'm for doing it, but we've got to make this tight from the start. If this operation were to blow, our asses and a lot of others would land right in jail, and for a lot longer than any of those Nixon honchos. We've got nothing to bargain with.

DDO: Oh, we do have a few files, Bob. Don't underestimate the power of a big fat file folder.

DDO: I had this report put together by econ research after our meeting last week. It's an estimate of the world economic slump, with a special look at U.S. problems. They see no chance of real recovery before 1977, maybe not even then. Unemployment's maybe going over ten percent, with 12 percent not out of the question. After Watergate and Vietnam, this depression will be enough to keep the Republicans permanently ruined.

DDM&S: Oh, I don't know Jack. Can't somebody like Reagan renounce the Nixon-Ford past and pull the party out of the ashes?

DDO: Would you vote to put Bonzo the Chimp's co-star in the White House? The opposition would crucify that fool.

DCI: Jack's right. Our man's got to be a Democrat, one we can compromise and then control. That's the only way to get a backlash going here against the people who sold out Vietnam, who got us in and couldn't win.

IG: What about the option of letting events take their course? It looks now like Wallace has a lock on the Democrats and we can lay back and help him along here and there to make sure. Then, when he's elected, we give him the usual peek at all the deep, dark secrets, parade out a few James Bond gadgets, and we have him in our pocket.

DCI: I realize you're playing devil's advocate, Stan, and I appreciate it, but the mere possibility of that Neanderthal as my leader, my country's leader, turns my stomach.

DDO: Wallace is a problem, though. We can't let him exploit anticommunism for isolationist purposes.

DCI: We've got to choose our candidate soon, get him compromised and get the psychological campaign going. Get him in the middle and force Wallace and Jerry to the edges.

May 1975

DCI: Jack and I have been working on organization for the past three weeks and I think we've got it pretty well plotted out on paper. First, we'll set up a central office here inside the Inspector General's office. Stan, as IG, you'll be responsible for this – keep it small, compartmented, out of the way. One or two offices with some desks, a filing safe and shredder – we don't want to use the normal burn chutes. Keep files to the bare minimum, too.

Bob, you'll have two top priorities: Get the Office of Finance to find some money – let's say $30,000,000 for the rest of '75 and $60,000,000 for the election year. Use proprietary income if you can, since it can be covered better. Try the airlines – Air America, Intermountain – or DoubleChek, Vanguard, one of the corporations. Next, get the communications people to set up an independent crypt system that we can use with appropriate field stations for this operation only.

DDM&S: Will we use the PBPRIME cryptonym?

DCI: Sure, why not? It signifies the entire geographic United States – it's suitably innocuous. Now, as to funds – Jack, you decide which of the foreign intelligence services can be used to channel the money back to us. You'll probably want to look in Latin America and Asia.

IG: Will the PBPRIME field setup be a bogus operation or part of the agency structure?

DCI: A little bit of both, Stan – they'll be special IG offices which you'll set up in the stations here run by the Domestic Operations Division. I figure that, with the inside operation, we'll need about 15 people, herein headquarters, plus 30 to 40to man the new IG offices around the country. Jack, you'll select these personnel from your most discreet and trusted people. Get men who've had covert experience in the field – branch chiefs at least, station chiefs if possible – and make sure they're eligible for retirement or close to it. We'll open special retirement accounts for them in case this thing blows.

Now, you're also going to need another 40 to 50 officers working outside, once the campaign gets started. You can recruit these, Jack, from officers who've recently retired, people who've worked in election and political-action operations in Latin America and the Far East.

DDO: I know just the man to handle it – Vern Shannon.

DCI: Brazil?

DDO: Right; he ran the entire anti-Goulart election operation out of Rio in '62 – handled a $20,000,000 campaign with about 1000 candidates running: senators, governors, legislators. That campaign led directly to Goulart getting thrown out by the military two years later. Shannon's a good man. Perfect for recruiting retirees for the outside operation.

IG: What are we talking about in terms of fronts?

DCI: Well, I think the priority need is for an umbrella political-action group, some kind of campaign to revive the Soviet and Communist danger. Something like the Crusade for Freedom – a mass movement. Set up a national office, regional chapters. Get the big names to sign on as patrons – not business people or bankers, they'll be kept in the background, but entertainers, athletes, intellectuals, writers, environmentalists, consumer advocates. Get as many media people as possible – TV, movie personalities. Then organizational support: scout groups, Legion, Shriners, NAACP, Rotary, AFL-CIO. Pump the need for revival of American spirit, patriotism, confidence – make it upbeat, positive. Then balance with strong warnings of the disintegration of our will to resist the creeping loss of freedom from Communist advance. Create tension, polarize – isolate opponents by forcing them into positions they are unprepared for. We've done it before.

Which reminds me, Jack, we're going to need the capacity to put out something like the Plan Z we used against Allende. Set up some private detective agencies to collect intelligence on the opposition that can be mixed with a little pure invention and put out forged papers.

DDO: I'll get a couple of retired technical-services people to help out.

DCI: Fine. Now I've got to get over to the White House or they'll be calling. God, it's slow going with Jerry. Poor retention, I'm afraid. I'll leave you people to work out the details.

October 1975

DDCI: The way we're moving on PBPRIME, the battle will be over before they're done with maneuvers. You're all doing a great job.

DDM&S: So's the candidate.

DCI: Yes, Henry Scooperman was the logical choice – popular Senator, ambitious, forceful, solid social-democrat record, no bad habits, great appearance, limited means –

DDO: And no child ever took candy so quickly. Using an Israeli cover agent to make the approach was perfect – QRTEST has legitimate credentials as a former chief of the Israeli service and Senator Scooperman has a strong pro-Israel foreign policy position; gave QRTEST plausible reason to offer support and gave our candidate the opening to rationalize foreign interest in his Presidential campaign. What's wrong with working with a close American ally whose interests are identical with ours? Scooperman needs money for his campaign and accepting Israeli donations is not much different from taking money from an American Zionist businessman. He'll never know the cash comes from us, since not even QRTEST knows for sure – our contacts with him are being handled by a former case officer in Tel Aviv, who now works for McDonnell Douglas.

DCI: S Scooperman's twice removed from us. Sounds good. Pass word to QRTE$T to give the Senator a lot of test assignments and make-work – speeches, position papers, personal appearance at a few meaningless banquets. We've got to get him used to taking orders.

Bob, any trouble on money? What sources are we using?

DDM&S: Got it all from the airline proprietaries, Air America mostly. They're putting cash – the first $30,000,000 – directly into 40-odd accounts in Zurich, Bern and Geneva.

DCI: All right, we've got the necessary cash on hand. Now to get to the individual liaison services. Next week, I'm going to send separate messages – "RYBAT/EYES ONLY" – to the chiefs of station in Bangkok, Santiago, Teheran, Djakarta, Brasilia, Montevideo, Jidda and Kinshasa, advising them that cash is on its way from Switzerland by special courier, earmarked for the domestic intelligence service in their country.

DDO: The cover being that it's an emergency fund for counterterror operations.

Sounds like I'm off on an eight-country inspection tour.

DCI: Starting in about ten days, Jack. I'll stagger the dispersals out of Switzerland so the couriers will be arriving in each country a couple of days before you get there. My message will tell the station chiefs to advise the penetration agents to hold the cash until contacted by an officer from headquarters.

DDM&S: And when Jack gets back, I'll deliver the cash into accounts we've opened around the country to finance the new IG operations in the DOD stations.

DCI: They're exclusively PBPRIME accounts – no strings to other IG operations or to domestic operations?

DDM&S: None. Only PBPRIME officers working under IG cover are authorized to draw.

February 1976

DCI: How're we handling Wallace?

DDO: We'll get him on medical records. We've got some pretty damaging stuff forged and ready for surfacing just before the first primary – material indicating he could go at any minute and that he had a form of meningitis that affected his brain somehow. This'll dovetail with a rumor campaign about how he's no damned good to his wife and that she may be looking elsewhere for her fun. We have some composite photographs that'll pretty effectively compromise Mrs. Wallace once his aides and financial supporters see them.

DCI: What about our Arab cover?

DDM&S: Oh, it worked out all right. We have plausible denial. The cash went straight from your safe to Copelen in Europe and then passed it to one of his Egyptian accounts.

June 1976

DCI: We need a crescendo effect building up to November. Don't forget my idea about having the coalition compare agency clandestine operations to the Boston Tea Party – that's a natural.

DDO: I wanted to tell you, too, that we've gotten two more House candidates compromised since last week. Both without a peep.

DCI: What's the total now?

DDO: Ten directly, from House incumbents, with preparations for 30 more. Altogether, we're getting into 70 House campaigns.

DCI: What're your covers?

DDM&S: Depends, corporations – those under Federal regulations – for bribes. Jealous husbands when women are involved.

IG: Where the approach isn't direct, we're using blackmail and black operations – damaging material in police files and newspaper records. We've got the detective agencies working on this and Jack has some people doing the same overseas, with foreign police records and newspapers.

DDO: The liaison services are helping out on this – planting black material like a report on a drug or morals arrest that coincides with a trip out target really made to a foreign country. We're planting this material on the ones who accept direct approaches, too, just in case it's needed later. Turns out Senator Scooperman took a trip to Yucatán with a couple of other fellows when he was 23, so there's an entry in the Mérida police records – the chief there has been with us since '63 – revealing that a certain Henry P. Scooperman of Portland, Oregon, was arrested in 1947 on charges of indecently assaulting a 12-year old native boy and was released after paying a fine of 2500 pesos.

September 1976

DDM&S: Next week, the coalition comes out publicly for Scooperman and will operate parallel to the Democratic Party campaign. We're keeping the Center for Democratic Action nonpartisan, concentrating on analysis and files.

DCI: Be careful that the coalition doesn't get absorbed into the Democratic Party structure. We may need it again later, as an independent organization.

November 1976

DCI: I'll be starting the usual briefings for the President-elect next week. I'll use the contact to take over personal direction of Scooperman from QRTEST. This will give us better control, fewer risks. I'm afraid our Israeli friend will have to be terminated. Jack, see that Black September gets enough data on his location and movements so that it can take care of this.

DDO: QRTEST's file will be in Beirut by Monday. We've got good penetration of the Palestinian crowd.[50]

It can't happen here? It has happened here many times over. And the late Phil Agee's crystal ball could have been trained ojn 2012. Substitute Mitt Romney for Henry Scooperman. Swap the Koch Brothers' Americans for Prosperity for

---

[50] Philip Agee, "CIA vs. USA: The Agency's Plot to Take Over America," *Oui*, September 1975.

the CIA's "coalition." And plug in Petraeus and pro-Romney elements into the clandestine operations in the fictional 1975- 1976 account and L'Affair Petraeus comes into greater focus.

The following words written by one of Petraeus's troops in Iraq should be read and remembered by every American and every citizen of the world who believes in democracy, the rule of law, and basic human rights:

> "Our country is amazing and a place worth holding dear, but very insidious things lurk in our government. Things we see here. Things you will never hear about. Things that you would never think could come of America. Be careful what you believe. Not everyone here dies the way the paper says they do. Some people aren't as brave as they say. Some people were more heroic than you will ever know."

Appendix

Members of Romney For President Military Advisory Council (or is that Emergency COMmunications CONtrol -- ECOMCON -- from *Seven Days in May*?)"

Admiral James B. Busey, USN, (Ret.)
General James T. Conway, USMC, (Ret.)
General Terrence R. Dake, USMC, (Ret)
Admiral James O. Ellis, USN, (Ret.)
Admiral Mark Fitzgerald, USM, (Ret.)
General Ronald R. Fogleman, USAF, (Ret)
Admiral S. Robert Foley Jr.,USN, (Ret.)
General Tommy Franks, USA, (Ret)
General Alfred Hansen, USAF, (Ret)
Admiral Ronald Jackson Hays, USN, (Ret)
Admiral Thomas Bibb Hayward, USN, (Ret)
General Chuck Albert Horner, USAF, (Ret)
Admiral Jerome LaMarr Johnson, USN, (Ret)
Admiral Timothy J. Keating, USN, (Ret)
General Paul X. Kelley, USMC, (Ret)
General William Kernan, USA, (Ret)
Admiral George E.R. Kinnear II, USN, (Ret)
General William L. Kirk, USAF, (Ret)
General James J. Lindsay, USA, (Ret)
General William R. Looney III, USAF, (Ret)
Admiral Hank Mauz, USN, (Ret)
General Robert Magnus, USMC, (Ret)
Admiral Paul David Miller, USN, (Ret)
General Robert C. Oaks, USAF, (Ret.)
General Henry Hugh Shelton, USA, (Ret)
General Lance Smith, USAF, (Ret)
Admiral Leighton Smith, Jr., USN, (Ret)
General Ronald W. Yates, USAF, (Ret)
Admiral Ronald J. Zlatoper, USN, (Ret)
Lieutenant General James Abrahamson, USAF, (Ret.)

Lieutenant General Teddy G. Allen, USA, (Ret.)
Lieutenant General Edgar Anderson, Jr., USAF, (Ret.)
Lieutenant General Marcus A. Anderson, USAF, (Ret.)
Lieutenant General Buck Bedard, USMC, (Ret.)
Vice Admiral A. Bruce Beran, USCG, (Ret.)
Vice Admiral Lyle Bien, USN, (Ret.)
Lieutenant General Harold Blot, USMC, (Ret.)
Lieutenant General H. Steven Blum, USA, (Ret.)
Vice Admiral Mike Bowman III, USN, (Ret.)
Vice Admiral Mike Bucchi, USN, (Ret.)
Lieutenant General Walter E. Buchanan III, USAF, (Ret.)
Lieutenant General Richard A. Burpee, USAF, (Ret.)
Lieutenant General William Campbell, USAF, (Ret.)
Lieutenant General James E. Chambers, USAF, (Ret.)
Vice Admiral Edward W. Clexton, Jr., USN, (Ret.)
Lieutenant General John B. Conaway, USAF, (Ret.)
Lieutenant General Marvin Covault, USA, (Ret.)
Vice Admiral Terry M. Cross, USCG, (Ret.)
Vice Admiral William Adam Dougherty, USN, (Ret.)
Lieutenant General Brett Dula, USAF, (Ret.)
Vice Admiral William Earner, USN, (Ret.)
Lieutenant General John S. Fairfield, USAF, (Ret.)
Lieutenant General Gordon E. Fornell, USAF, (Ret.)
Vice Admiral David Frost, USN, (Ret.)
Vice Admiral Henry C. Giffin III, USN, (Ret.)
Vice Admiral Peter M. Hekman, USN, (Ret.)
Vice Admiral Richard D. Herr, USCG, (Ret.)
Lieutenant General Thomas J Hickey, USAF, (Ret.)
Lieutenant General Walter S. Hogle, Jr., USAF, (Ret.)
Lieutenant General Ronald W. Iverson, USAF, (Ret.)
Lieutenant General Donald W. Jones, USA, (Ret.)
Vice Admiral Douglas J. Katz, USN, (Ret.)
Lieutenant General Jay W. Kelley, USAF, (Ret.)
Vice Admiral Tom Kilcline, USN, (Ret.)
Lieutenant General Timothy A. Kinnan, USAF, (Ret.)
Vice Admiral Harold Koenig, M.D., USN, (Ret.)
Vice Admiral Albert H. Konetzni, USN, (Ret.)
Lieutenant General Buford Derald Lary, USAF, (Ret.)
Lieutenant General Frank Libutti, USMC, (Ret.)
Vice Admiral Stephen Loftus, USN, (Ret.)
Vice Admiral Michael Malone, USN, (Ret.)

Vice Admiral Edward H. Martin, USN, (Ret.)
Vice Admiral John J. Mazach, USN, (Ret.)
Vice Admiral Justin D. McCarthy, USN, (Ret.)
Vice Admiral William McCauley, USN, (Ret.)
Lieutenant General Fred McCorkle, USMC, (Ret.)
Lieutenant General Thomas G. McInerney, USAF, (Ret.)
Vice Admiral Joseph S. Mobley, USN, (Ret.)
Lieutenant General Carol Mutter, USMC, (Ret.)
Lieutenant General Ira Owens, USA, (Ret.)
Lieutenant General Dave R. Palmer, USA, (Ret.)
Vice Admiral John Theodore "Ted" Parker, USN, (Ret.)
Lieutenant General Garry L. Parks, USMC, (Ret.)
Lieutenant General Charles Henry "Chuck" Pitman, USMC, (Ret.)
Lieutenant General Steven R. Polk, USAF, (Ret.)
Vice Admiral William E. Ramsey, USN, (Ret.)
Lieutenant General Joseph J. Redden, USAF, (Ret.)
Lieutenant General Clifford H. "Ted" Rees, Jr., USAF, (Ret.)
Lieutenant General Edward Rowny, USA (Ret.)
Vice Admiral Dutch Schultz, USN, (Ret.)
Lieutenant General Charles J. Searock, Jr., USAF, (Ret.)
Lieutenant General E. G. "Buck" Shuler, USAF, (Ret.)
Lieutenant General Alexander M. "Rusty" Sloan, USAF, (Ret.)
Vice Admiral Edward M. Straw, USN, (Ret.)
Lieutenant General David J. Teal, USAF, (Ret.)
Lieutenant General Billy M. Thomas, USA, (Ret.)
Vice Admiral Donald C. "Deese" Thompson, USCG, (Ret.)
Vice Admiral Alan S. Thompson, USN, (Ret.)
Lieutenant General Herman O. "Tommy" Thomson, USAF, (Ret.)
Vice Admiral Howard B. Thorsen, USCG, (Ret.)
Lieutenant General William Thurman, USAF, (Ret.)
Lieutenant General Robert Allen "R.A." Tiebout, USMC, (Ret.)
Vice Admiral John B. Totushek, USNR, (Ret.)
Lieutenant General George J. Trautman, USMC, (Ret.)
Lieutenant General Garry R. Trexler, USAF, (Ret.)
Vice Admiral Jerry O. Tuttle, USN, (Ret.)
Lieutenant General Claudius "Bud" Watts, USAF, (Ret.)
Lieutenant General William "Bill" Welser, USAF, (Ret.)
Lieutenant General Thad A. Wolfe, USAF, (Ret.)
Lieutenant General C. Norman Wood, USAF, (Ret.)
Lieutenant General Michael W. Wooley, USAF, (Ret.)
Lieutenant General Richard "Rick" Zilmer, USMC, (Ret.)

Major General Chris Adams, USAF, (Ret.)
Rear Admiral Henry Amos, USN (Ret.)
Major General Nora Alice Astafan, USAF, (Ret.)
Major General Almon Bowen Ballard, USAF, (Ret.)
Major General James F. Barnette, USAF, (Ret.)
Major General Robert W. Barrow, USAF, (Ret.)
Rear Admiral John R. Batlzer, USN, (Ret.)
Rear Admiral Jon W. Bayless, USN, (Ret.)
Major General John E. Bianchi, USA, (Ret.)
Major General David F. Bice, USMC, (Ret.)
Rear Admiral Linda J. Bird, USN, (Ret.)
Rear Admiral James H. Black, USN, (Ret.)
Rear Admiral Peter A. Bondi, USN, (Ret.)
Major General John L. Borling, USAF, (Ret.)
Major General Tom Braaten, USMC, (Ret.)
Major General Patrick H. Brady, USA, (Ret.)
Major General Robert J. Brandt, USA, (Ret.)
Rear Admiral Jerry C. Breast, USN, (Ret.)
Rear Admiral Bruce B. Bremner, USN, (Ret.)
Rear Admiral Thomas F. Brown III, USN, (Ret.)
Major General David P. Burford, USA, (Ret.)
Rear Admiral John F. Calvert, USN, (Ret.)
Rear Admiral Jay A. Campbell, USN, (Ret.)
Major General Henry Canterbury, USAF, (Ret.)
Rear Admiral James J. Carey, USN, (Ret.)
Rear Admiral Nevin Carr, USN, (Ret.)
Rear Admiral Stephen K. Chadwick, USN, (Ret.)
Rear Admiral W. Lewis Chatham, USN, (Ret.)
Major General Jeffrey G. Cliver, USAF, (Ret.)
Rear Admiral Casey Coane, USN, (Ret.)
Rear Admiral Isaiah C. Cole, USN, (Ret.)
Major General Stephen Condon, USAF, (Ret.)
Major General Richard C. Cosgrave, USANG, (Ret.)
Rear Admiral Robert Cowley, USN, (Ret.)
Major General J.T. Coyne, USMC, (Ret.)
Rear Admiral Robert C. Crates, USN, (Ret.)
Major General Tommy F. Crawford, USAF, (Ret.)
Major General Gerald A. Daniel, USAF, (Ret.)
Rear Admiral James P. Davidson, USN, (Ret.)
Rear Admiral Kevin F. Delaney, USN, (Ret.)
Major General James D. Delk, USA, (Ret.)

Major General Robert E. Dempsey, USAF, (Ret.)
Rear Admiral Jay Ronald Denney, USNR, (Ret.)
Major General Robert S. Dickman, USAF, (Ret.)
Rear Admiral James C. Doebler, USN, (Ret.)
Major General Douglas O. Dollar, USA, (Ret.)
Major General Hunt Downer, USA, (Ret.)
Major General Thomas A. Dyches, USAF, (Ret.)
Major General Jay T. Edwards, USAF, (Ret.)
Major General John R. Farrington, USAF, (Ret.)
Rear Admiral Francis L. Filipiak, USN, (Ret.)
Rear Admiral James H. Flatley III, USN, (Ret.)
Major General Charles Fletcher, USA, (Ret.)
Major General Bobby O. Floyd, USAF, (Ret.)
Rear Admiral Veronica Froman, USN, (Ret.)
Rear Admiral Vance H. Fry, USN, (Ret.)
Rear Admiral R. Byron Fuller, USN, (Ret.)
Rear Admiral George M. Furlong, USN, (Ret.)
Rear Admiral Frank Gallo, USN, (Ret.)
Rear Admiral Ben F. Gaumer, USN, (Ret.)
Rear Admiral Harry E. Gerhard Jr., USN, (Ret.)
Major General Daniel J. Gibson, USAF, (Ret.)
Rear Admiral Andrew A. Giordano, USN, (Ret.)
Major General Richard N. Goddard, USAF, (Ret.)
Rear Admiral Fred Golove, USCGR, (Ret.)
Rear Admiral Harold Eric Grant, USN, (Ret.)
Major General Jeff Grime, USAF, (Ret.)
Major General Robert Kent Guest, USA, (Ret.)
Major General Tim Haake, USAR, (Ret.)
Major General Otto K. Habedank, USAF, (Ret.)
Rear Admiral Thomas F. Hall, USN, (Ret.)
Rear Admiral Donald P. Harvey, USN, (Ret.)
Major General Leonard W. Hegland, USAF, (Ret.)
Rear Admiral John Hekman, USN, (Ret.)
Major General John A. Hemphill, USA, (Ret.)
Rear Admiral Larry Hereth, USCG, (Ret.)
Major General Wilfred Hessert, USAF, (Ret.)
Rear Admiral Don Hickman, USN, (Ret.)
Major General Geoffrey Higginbotham, USMC, (Ret.)
Rear Admiral Grant Hollett, USN, (Ret.)
Major General Jerry D. Holmes, USAF, (Ret.)
Major General Weldon F. Honeycutt, USA, (Ret.)

Rear Admiral Steve Israel, USN, (Ret.)
Major General James T. Jackson, USA, (Ret.)
Rear Admiral John S. Jenkins, USN, (Ret.)
Rear Admiral Tim Jenkins, USN, (Ret.)
Rear Admiral Ron Jesberg, USN, (Ret.)
Rear Admiral Pierce J. Johnson, USN, (Ret.)
Rear Admiral Steven B. Kantrowitz, USN, (Ret.)
Rear Admiral John T. Kavanaugh, USN, (Ret.)
Major General George W. Keefe, ANG, (Ret.)
Rear Admiral Stephen T. Keith, USN, (Ret.)
Major General Dennis M. Kenneally, USA, (Ret.)
Major General Michael Kerby, USAF, (Ret.)
Rear Admiral David Kunkel, USCG, (Ret.)
Major General Geoffrey C. Lambert, USA, (Ret.)
Rear Admiral Arthur Langston, USN, (Ret.)
Rear Admiral Thomas G. Lilly, USN, (Ret.)
Major General James E. Livingston, USMC, (Ret.)
Major General Al Logan, USAF, (Ret.)
Major General John D. Logeman Jr., USAF, (Ret.)
Rear Admiral Noah H. Long Jr, USNR, (Ret.)
Rear Admiral Don Loren, USN, (Ret.)
Major General Andy Love, USAF, (Ret.)
Rear Admiral Thomas C. Lynch, USN, (Ret.)
Rear Admiral Steven Wells Maas, USN, (Ret.)
Major General Robert M. Marquette, USAF, (Ret.)
Rear Admiral Larry Marsh, USN, (Ret.)
Major General Clark W. Martin, USAF, (Ret.)
Major General William M. Matz, USN, (Ret.)
Rear Admiral Gerard Mauer, USN, (Ret.)
Major General James C. McCombs, USAF, (Ret.)
Rear Admiral William J. McDaniel, MD, USN, (Ret.)
Rear Admiral E.S. McGinley II, USN, (Ret.)
Rear Admiral Henry C. McKinney, USN, (Ret.)
Major General Robert Messerli, USAF, (Ret.)
Major General Douglas S. Metcalf, USAF, (Ret.)
Rear Admiral James E. Miller, USN, (Ret.)
Rear Admiral John W. Miller, USN, (Ret.)
Rear Admiral Patrick David Moneymaker, USN, (Ret.)
Major General Mario Montero, USA, (Ret.)
Rear Admiral Douglas M. Moore, USN, (Ret.)
Major General Walter Bruce Moore, USA, (Ret.)

Major General William Moore, USA, (Ret.)
Major General Burton R. Moore, USAF, (Ret.)
Rear Admiral James A. Morgart, USN, (Ret.)
Major General Stanton R. Musser, USAF, (Ret.)
Rear Admiral John T. Natter, USN, (Ret.)
Brigadier General Michael Neil, USMCR, (Ret.)
Rear Admiral Edward Nelson, Jr., USCG, (Ret.)
Major General Robert A. Nester, USAF, (Ret.)
Major General George W. Norwood, USAF, (Ret.)
Rear Admiral Robert C. Olsen, USN, (Ret.)
Rear Admiral James D. Olson, USN, (Ret.)
Major General Raymund E. O'Mara, USAF, (Ret.)
Rear Admiral Robert S. Owens, USN, (Ret.)
Rear Admiral John F. Paddock, USN, (Ret.)
Major General Robert W. Paret, USAF, (Ret.)
Rear Admiral Robert O. Passmore, USN, (Ret.)
Major General Earl G. Peck, USAF, (Ret.)
Major General Richard E. Perraut Jr., USAF, (Ret.)
Major General Gerald F. Perryman, USAF, (Ret.)
Rear Admiral W.W. Pickavance, USN, (Ret.)
Rear Admiral John J. Prendergast, USN, (Ret.)
Rear Admiral Fenton F. Priest, USN, (Ret.)
Major General David C. Ralston, USA, (Ret.)
Major General Bentley B. Rayburn, USAF, (Ret.)
Rear Admiral Harold Rich, USN , (Ret.)
Rear Admiral Roland Rieve, USN, (Ret.)
Rear Admiral Tommy F. Rinard, USN , (Ret.)
Major General Richard H. Roellig, USAF, (Ret.)
Rear Admiral Michael S. Roesner, USN, (Ret.)
Major General Davis Rohr, USAF, (Ret.)
Rear Admiral William J. Ryan, USN, (Ret.)
Major General Loran C. Schnaidt, USAF, (Ret.)
Major General Carl Schneider, USAF , (Ret.)
Major General John P. Schoeppner, Jr., USAF, (Ret.)
Major General Edison E. Scholes, USAF, (Ret.)
Rear Admiral Robert H. Shumaker, USN, (Ret.)
Rear Admiral William S. Schwob, USCG, (Ret.)
Major General David J. Scott, USAF, (Ret.)
Rear Admiral Hugh P. Scott, USN, (Ret.)
Major General Richard Secord, USAF, (Ret.)
Rear Admiral William H. Shawcross, USN, (Ret.)

Major General Joseph K. Simeone, USAF and ANG , (Ret.)
Major General Darwin Simpson, ANG , (Ret.)
Rear Admiral Greg Slavonic, USN , (Ret.)
Rear Admiral David Oliver "D.O." Smart, USNR, (Ret.)
Major General David R. Smith, USAF (Ret.)
Major General Richard D. Smith, USAF, (Ret.)
Major General Donald Bruce Smith, USAF, (Ret.)
Rear Admiral Paul O. Soderberg, USN, (Ret.)
Major General Stan Spears, ANG, (Ret.)
Rear Admiral Robert H. "Bob" Spiro, USN, (Ret.)
Major General Henry B. Stelling, Jr., USAF, (Ret.)
Rear Admiral Daniel H. Stone, USN, (Ret.)
Brigadier General Joseph Stringham, USA, (Ret.)
Major General Ansel M. Stroud, Jr., USA, (Ret.)
Major General William A. Studer, USAF, (Ret.)
Rear Admiral Hamlin Tallent, USN, (Ret.)
Brigadier General Hugh Banks Tant III, USA, (Ret.)
Major General Larry S. Taylor, USMC, (Ret.)
Major General J.B. Taylor, USA, (Ret.)
Major General Thomas R. Tempel, USA , (Ret.)
Major General Richard L. Testa, USAF, (Ret.)
Rear Admiral Jere Thompson, USN (Ret.)
Rear Admiral Byron E. Tobin, USN, (Ret.)
Rear Admiral Roger W. Triftshauser, USNR, (Ret.)
Major General Larry Twitchell, USAF, (Ret.)
Major General Russell L. Violett, USAF, (Ret.)
Major General John G. Waggener, USA, (Ret.)
Rear Admiral Edward K. Walker, Jr., USN, (Ret.)
Major General David E.B. "DEB" Ward, USAF, (Ret.)
Major General Charles J. Wax, USAF, (Ret.)
Rear Admiral Donald Weatherson, USN, (Ret.)
Major General John Welde, USAF, (Ret.)
Major General Gary Whipple, USA , (Ret.)
Rear Admiral James B. Whittaker, USN, (Ret.)
Rear Admiral Charles Williams, USN, (Ret.)
Rear Admiral H. Denny Wisely, USN, (Ret.)
Rear Admiral Theodore J. Wojnar, USCG, (Ret.)
Rear Admiral George R. Worthington, USN, (Ret.)
Brigadier General Arthur Abercrombie, USA, (Ret.)
Brigadier General John R. Allen, USAF, (Ret.)
Brigadier General Loring R. Astorino, USAF, (Ret.)

Brigadier General Richard Averitt, USA, (Ret.)
Brigadier General Garry S. Bahling, USANG, (Ret.)
Brigadier General Donald E. Barnhart, USAF, (Ret.)
Brigadier General Charles L. Bishop, USAF, (Ret.)
Brigadier General Clayton Bridges, USAF, (Ret.)
Brigadier General Jeremiah J. Brophy, USA, (Ret.)
Brigadier General R. Thomas Browning, USAF, (Ret.)
Brigadier General David A. Brubaker, USAF, (Ret.)
Brigadier General Chalmers R. Carr, USAF, (Ret.)
Brigadier General Fred F. Castle, USAFR, (Ret.)
Brigadier General Robert V. Clements, USAF, (Ret.)
Brigadier General Christopher T Cline, USAR, (Ret.)
Brigadier General George Peyton Cole, Jr., USAF, (Ret.)
Brigadier General Richard A. Coleman, USAF, (Ret.)
Brigadier General Mike Cushman, USAF, (Ret.)
Brigadier General Peter Dawkins, USA, (Ret.)
Brigadier General Sam. G. DeGeneres, USAF, (Ret.)
Brigadier General George Demers, USAF, (Ret.)
Brigadier General Howard G. DeWolf, USAF, (Ret.)
Brigadier General Arthur F. Diehl, USAF, (Ret.)
Brigadier General David Bob Edmonds, USAF, (Ret.)
Brigadier General Anthony Farrington, USAF, (Ret.)
Brigadier General Norm Gaddis, USAF, (Ret.)
Brigadier General E.J. Giering III, USA, (Ret.)
Brigadier General Robert H. Harkins, USAF, (Ret.)
Brigadier General Thomas W. Honeywill, USAF, (Ret.)
Brigadier General Stanley V. Hood, USAF, (Ret.)
Brigadier General James J. Hourin, USAF, (Ret.)
Brigadier General Jack C. Ihle, USAF, (Ret.)
Brigadier General Thomas G. Jeter, USAF, (Ret.)
Brigadier General William Herbert Johnson, USAF, (Ret.)
Brigadier General Kenneth F. Keller, USAF, (Ret.)
Brigadier General Wayne W. Lambert, USAF, (Ret.)
Brigadier General Jerry L. Laws, USA, (Ret.)
Brigadier General Thomas J. Lennon, USAF, (Ret.)
Brigadier General John M. Lotz, USAF, (Ret.)
Brigadier General Robert S. Mangum, USA, (Ret.)
Brigadier General Frank Martin, USAF, (Ret.)
Brigadier General Joe Mensching, USAF, (Ret.)
Brigadier General Richard L. Meyer, USAF, (Ret.)
Brigadier General Lawrence A. Mitchell, USAF, (Ret.)

Brigadier General Michael P. Mulqueen, USMC, (Ret.)
Brigadier General Ben Nelson, Jr., USAF, (Ret.)
Brigadier General Jack W. Nicholson, USA, (Ret.)
Brigadier General Maria C. Owens, USAF, (Ret.)
Brigadier General Dave Papak, USMC, (Ret.)
Brigadier General Gary A. Pappas, USANG, (Ret.)
Brigadier General John G. Pappas, USA, (Ret.)
Brigadier General Robert V. Paschon, USAF, (Ret.)
Brigadier General Allen K. Rachel, USAF, (Ret.)
Brigadier General Jon Reynolds, USAF, (Ret.)
Brigadier General Edward F. Rodriguez, Jr., USAFR, (Ret.)
Brigadier General Harold W. Rudolph, USAF, (Ret.)
Brigadier General Roger Scearce, USA, (Ret.)
Brigadier General Dennis Schulstad, USAFR, (Ret.)
Brigadier General John Serur, USAF, (Ret.)
Brigadier General Joseph L. Shaefer, USAF, (Ret.)
Brigadier General Graham Shirley, USAF, (Ret.)
Brigadier General Raymond Shulstad, USAF, (Ret.)
Brigadier General Stan Smith, USAF, (Ret.)
Brigadier General Ralph S. Smith, USAF, (Ret.)
Brigadier General Donald Smith, USA, (Ret.)
Brigadier General David M. Snyder, USAF, (Ret.)
Brigadier General Michael Joseph Tashjian, USAF, (Ret.)
Brigadier General Richard Louis Ursone, USA, (Ret.)
Brigadier General Earl Van Inwegen, USAF, (Ret.)
Brigadier General Robert V. Woods, USAF (Ret.)
Brigadier General Terrence P. Woods, USAF, (Ret.)
Brigadier General Mitchell Zais, USA, (Ret.)
Brigadier General Allan Ralph Zenowitz, USA, (Ret.)

(11/15/2012) Bob Buckhorn - 10/30 2-5pm

From: "Jill G. Kelley" <skelleymd@yahoo.com>
To: Bob Buckhorn <Bob.Buckhorn@ci.tampa.fl.us>
Date: 10/9/2011 9:26 PM
Subject: 10/30 2-5pm

Bob & Cathy,
Hello, it was great seeing at Gen Mattis' home
Scott, Me & the girls are en route home from South Beach
(so fun!)

I wanted to invite you and your family to join us for our daughter Caroline's 6th birthday party on my front lawn
Sunday 10/30 from 2-5pm

The age group will vary since everyone is bringing their siblings, so I made activities for all age groups, including a live DJ!
(and an Open Bar for "us kids"! hehe! :-)

You'll recognize many faces of friends stopping by (without kids)
Love to have you guys join us!
Your friend,
Jill
ps I'll be in DC this weekend with Petreaus, but let's set up a double date when I return!

Sent from my iPhone; Please pardon typos and brevity.

CHADBOURNE
& PARKE LLP

Abbe D. Lowell
direct tel +1 202 974 5605
adlowell@chadbourne.com

November 27, 2012

VIA EMAIL - W.Stephen.Muldrow@usdoj.gov

W. Stephen Muldrow, Esquire
Assistant United States Attorney
Middle District of Florida
U.S. Attorney's Office
400 North Tampa St
Suite 3200
Tampa, FL 33602

Re: <u>Dr. Scott and Jill Kelley</u>

Dear Mr. Muldrow:

During earlier conversations, I had mentioned to you and to Agent Adam Malone of the Federal Bureau of Investigation my concern about leaks that had occurred in the above-referenced matter. These leaks most certainly had to come, at least in part, from government sources. The earliest and best example of the leaks would be the release to the media of the names of my clients. As you know, there are several rules and laws that seek to protect United States citizens against such leaks. Among these is the Privacy Act, which would be particularly applicable to the release of the Kelleys' names. I presume, but do not know, that people in the FBI were responsible for leaking information about the FBI agent who allegedly sent inappropriate photos to Ms. Kelley (a photo that was, in the end, obviously a joke).

I write to ask whether the DOJ is investigating these leaks and potential infringements upon the Kelleys' privacy, including but not limited to violations of the Privacy Act, as part of its current work. I also wanted to let you know that, on behalf of the Kelleys, we are researching these issues to advise them of their right to pursue these issues civilly. You no doubt have seen the tremendous attention that the Kelleys have received in the media. All they did to receive this attention was to let law enforcement know that they had been the subjects of inappropriate and potentially threatening behavior by someone else. I appreciate your consideration and will let you know if we find other information.

Sincerely,

Abbe David Lowell

ADL/fn

Index

101st Airborne Division, 6, 44
Abedin, Huma, 52
Abizaid, Gen. John, 52, 53
Abu Nidal Organization, 69
Aerocom, 83, 84
AFRICOM
  U.S. Africa Command, 19, 24, 26, 40, 41, 42
Agee, Phil, 98, 99, 105
Agility, 81, 82
Ailes, Roger, 27, 31, 32
AIPAC
  American Israel Public Affairs Committee, 12, 17, 18, 24
Akkadian Private Ventures, LLC, 43
Al Qaeda, 17, 20, 50
al Sadr, Muqtada, 70, 71, 74, 93
al Zarqawi, Abu Musab, 73
Albright, Madeleine, 14
Allen, Gen. John, 38, 44, 52
Allred, Gloria, 63
al-Maliki, Nouri, 72
American Enterprise Institute
  AEI, 77, 90
Ames, Aldrich, 48
Ansar al-Sharia, 17, 20
Argo, 5, 51
Assange, Julian, 58
Bacile, Sam
  aka, Nakoula Basseley Nakoula, Abnob Bakoula Basseley, Joseph Nasralla Abdelmasih, 17, 18
Baer, Robert, 59, 60
Baier, Bret, 32
Benghazi, 1, 3, 7, 8, 9, 11, 13, 17, 18, 19, 24, 25, 26, 34, 35, 37, 40, 47, 49, 51, 56, 58, 59, 68, 86
Berger, Lawrence, 13
Berger, Sandy, 13
Biden, Joe, 42
bin Laden, Osama, 8
Blackwater, 6, 39
Blue Cloud Film Ranch, 17
Boehner, John, 12, 23

Booz Allen Hamilton, 80
Bout, Viktor, 83, 84, 85
Bremer, Paul "Jerry", 42, 44
Broadwell, Paula, 3, 5, 14, 26, 35, 38, 44, 52, 58, 63
Brownell, Robert
  aka, Alan Roberts, 17
Buckhorn, Bob, 64
Bullock, Bob, 61
Bullock, Ronald, 14
Bush, George H. W., 7
Butler, Smedley, 35
Camp Arifjan, 90
Cantor, Eric, 12, 13, 14, 17, 23, 34, 35, 39, 40, 46, 47, 58, 62
Capitol City Group, 44
Carter, Jimmy, 5, 6, 7, 8, 9, 11, 13, 18, 23, 24, 37, 47, 49, 51, 68
Casey, Gen. George, 71, 74
Casey, William, 48, 110
CBS, 17
CENTCOM
  U.S. Central Command, 4, 13, 39, 42, 53, 62
Chalabi, Ahmed, 77, 82, 92
CIA
  Central Intelligence Agency, 3, 5, 6, 7, 8, 12, 19, 21, 22, 23, 24, 26, 34, 35, 38, 47, 48, 49, 51, 52, 53, 56, 58, 59, 60, 62, 68, 69, 70
Clapper, Gen. James, 7, 9, 23, 34
Clark, Wesley, 31
Clem, Todd, 64
Clooney, George, 15, 51
Coalition Provisional Authority, 42, 44
CODEL
  Congressional delegation, 12
Cohen, Barry, 41
Condit, Gary, 41, 45, 46, 47
Cosumano, Joseph, 81
CRITIC
  message, 19, 22
Crocker, Ryan, 71
Custer Battles, 6
D'Agostino, Ryan, 30, 31

Dax, Tim, 17, 18
Defense Clandestine Service, 28
Dempsey, Gen. Martin, 22, 23, 34, 40, 111
Denham, Jeff, 12
Deutch, John, 48, 49
Diplomatic Security Service, 20
Duelfer, Charles, 79
Dulles, Allen, 48, 60
Edwards, John, 41
Erdogan, Recep Tayyip, 20
Fallon, Adm. William, 12, 66, 95
FBI
    Federal Bureau of Investigation, 5, 6, 7, 12, 13, 14, 15, 16, 18, 23, 34, 35, 38, 39, 40, 46, 53, 58, 59, 60, 61, 62, 69
Feinstein, Dianne, 6, 23
Feith, Douglas, 77
Fidan, Hakan, 20
Foggo, Kyle "Dusty", 49
Foreign Leaders Program, 53
Gaouette, Adm. Charles, 24, 35, 40
Gates, Robert, 7, 27, 49, 66
Geller, Pam, 17
Global Linguist Solutions LLC, 25
Glover Park Group, 63
Goss, Porter, 49, 56, 57
Gottlieb, Michael J., 63
Grimm, Michael, 12
Halliburton, 88, 94
Ham, Carter, 24
Ham, Gen. Carter, 24
Harman, Jane, 23
Harrington, Gerald, 44
Hartman, Cdr. Ray, 40
Harward, Vice Adm., 39, 42
Hayden, Gen. Michael, 38, 49, 60
Heye, Doug, 12, 14
Hitselberger, James, 24, 25
Holder, Eric, 12, 46
Horowitz, David, 17
Hugel, Max, 48
Humphries, Frederick W., 13, 14, 40, 46, 53, 58, 62
Hunter, Rielle, 41
Industry Sales Tax Solutions, LLC, 45
Innocence of Muslims, 17, 18, 49, 68

International Visitor Leadership Program, 53
Israel, Jimmy, 17
Issa, Darrell, 20
Ivens, Stephen, 15, 16, 17, 18, 23, 58
Joint Special Operations Command, 11
Jones, Gen. James, 66
Jundallah, 70
Kagan, Robert, 96
Kelley, Jill, 11, 13, 38, 41, 44, 46, 52, 53, 54, 55, 56, 62, 64
Kellogg, Brown & Root, 81, 84, 88
Kerry, John, 44
Knowlton, Gen. William, 4
Kranz, Paul, 47
Kranz, Stephen, 45
KRISS Arms, 39
Kristol, William, 34
Kubasik, Christopher, 38
Kubisek, Christopher, 59
Kusa, Musa, 22
L3 Communications, 25
Lantos, Tom, 6
Lee Dynamics International, 91
Levy, Chandra, 41, 45, 46
Lieberman, Joe, 32, 88
Lockeed Martin, 59
Loeb, Vernon, 5, 10
Lowell, Abbe, 41, 63
MacArthur, Douglas, 35, 36, 78
MacDill Air Force Base, 11, 13, 14, 38, 41, 53, 54, 62, 63, 64
Mahdavi, Fereidoun, 77
Mahdi Army, 70, 71, 72, 73, 74, 75, 85
Marshack, Megan, 11
Massa, Eric, 29, 30, 31
Mattis, Gen. James, 42
May, Clifford, 43
McCain, John, 4, 6, 48, 52
McCarthy, Kevin, 12, 109
McChrystal, Stanley, 65, 66
McFarland, Kathleen T. (K.T.), 27, 31, 32, 33
Meese, Michael, 95
MEK. *See* Mohajedin-e-Khalq
Merrill, Phil, 44
Microsoft, 38

MNSTC-I
  Multi-National Security Transition Command - Iraq, 6
Mohajedin-e-Khaliq
  MEK, 76
Mossad, 17, 21, 23, 69, 70
Mueller, Robert, 12, 46
Muldrow, W. Stephen, 41
Mullen, Adm. Michael, 62, 67
Murdoch, Rupert, 27, 32, 34
National Conference of State Legislatures, 27
Netanyahu, Binyamin, 8, 14, 16, 47
Nordstrom, Eric, 20
NSA
  National Security Agency, 5, 22, 38, 39, 60
Nuland, Victoria, 96
Obama, Barack, 1, 4, 5, 6, 8, 9, 11, 13, 15, 16, 17, 18, 19, 23, 25, 26, 37, 38, 42, 45, 46, 47, 48, 49, 51, 52, 56, 58, 59, 63, 68
October Surprise, 5, 6, 8, 13, 14, 47, 49, 68
Operation Grand Bahman, 79
OPERATION JACKAL STONE, 24
Palfrey, Deborah Jeane, 47, 56
Panetta, Leon, 9, 22, 23, 34, 40, 42, 49
Paramount, 17
Park, Tongsun, 54
Perry, Mark, 70
Perry, Rick, 60, 61, 62
Petraeus, David, 3, 4, 5, 6, 7, 8, 10, 11, 12, 13, 14, 15, 17, 19, 20, 23, 24, 25, 26, 34, 35, 37, 38, 39, 40, 41, 42, 44, 46, 47, 48, 49, 51, 52, 53, 54, 56, 58, 59, 62, 63, 64, 68
Petraeus, Holly, 4, 52
Pomerance, Ruth, 18
Prieto, Rafael, 15, 16, 17, 18, 23, 45, 46, 58
PWC Logistics, 82
Qaddafi, Muammar, 9, 19, 20, 21, 22
Quayle, Ben, 12
Rampton, Greg, 60, 61
Reed, Tom, 12
Reichert, Dave, 12, 13, 23, 39, 46, 53, 58
Reinfeldt, Fredrik, 56, 58
Ressam, Ahmed, 13
Rice, Susan, 68
Rockefeller, Nelson, 11
Rogers, Mike, 23
Romney, Mitt, 5, 6, 8, 9, 11, 14, 15, 18, 19, 23, 24, 26, 35, 37, 38, 44, 47, 49, 52, 59, 68, 87, 107
Ross, Dennis, 77, 96
Rove, Karl, 3, 8, 26, 27, 35, 37, 52, 56, 58, 59, 60, 61, 62
Secord, Richard, 87, 113
Senor, Dan, 8, 14, 37, 44
Sherman, Brad, 43
Sinclair, Brig. Gen. Jeffrey, 39
Sinofsky, Steven, 38, 39
Sixth Fleet, 40
Smith, Sean, 19
Sombres, Steven, 12, 46
Southerland, Steve, 12
Special Operations Command, 62
Spencer, Robert, 17, 41
Stavridis, Adm. James, 42
Stevens, Christopher, 19, 22, 23, 24, 26, 34, 38, 50, 58, 68
Summit of the Americas, 16, 45
Talabani, Jalal, 73, 77
Tallil Air Base, 70, 71, 72, 73
Taos, Inc., 81, 82, 83
Titan Corporation, 25
US Investigations Services, 92
USS John Stennis, 24
USS Liberty, 67
Victor, Adam, 41
Ward, Gen. William E. "Kip", 114
Ward, Gen. William E. "Kip", 40, 42
Washington Institute for Near East Policy
  WINEP, 77
Weiner, Anthony, 52
Westhusing, Ted, 91, 92
Whitehouse, Sheldon, 44
Williams & Connolly, 64
Williams, Ted Capt., 40
Wolfe, Grayson, 42, 43
Wolfe, Paul G., 43
Woodward, Bob, 26
Woolsey, James, 48

About the Author

Wayne Madsen is a Washington, DC-based investigative journalist, author and syndicated columnist. He has written for *The Village Voice, The Progressive, Counterpunch, In These Times,* and *The American Conservative*. His columns have appeared in *The Miami Herald, Houston Chronicle, Philadelphia Inquirer, Columbus Dispatch, Sacramento Bee,* and *Atlanta Journal-Constitution,* among others.

Madsen is the author of *The Handbook of Personal Data Protection* (London: Macmillan, 1992), an acclaimed reference book on international data protection law; *Genocide and Covert Operations in Africa 1993-1999* (Edwin Mellen Press, 1999); co-author of *America's Nightmare: The Presidency of George Bush II* (Dandelion, 2003); author of *Jaded Tasks: Big Oil, Black Ops & Brass Plates, Overthrow a Fascist Regime on $15 a Day.* (Trine Day), *Decade of Death: Secret Wars and Genocide in Africa 1993-2003,* and *The Manufacturing of a President: The CIA's Insertion of Barack H. Obama, Jr. Into the White House.*

Madsen has been a regular contributor on RT. He has also been a frequent political and national security commentator on Fox News and has also appeared on ABC, NBC, CBS, PBS, CNN, BBC, Al Jazeera, and MS-NBC. Madsen has taken on Bill O'Reilly and Sean Hannity on their television shows. He has been invited to testify as a witness before the US House of Representatives, the UN Criminal Tribunal for Rwanda, and a terrorism investigation panel of the French government.

As a U.S. Naval Officer, he served in anti-submarine warfare, telecommunications, and computer security positions. He subsequently was assigned to the National Security Agency. Madsen was a Senior Fellow for the Electronic Privacy Information Center (EPIC), a privacy advocacy organization.

Madsen is a member of the Society of Professional Journalists (SPJ) and the National Press Club.